PENGUIN
WATCHING IN

Artemis Cooper is the author of *Cairo in the War* and editor of two collections of letters, *A Durable Fire*, the letters of Duff and Diana Cooper, and *Mr Wu and Mrs Stitch*, the letters of Evelyn Waugh and Diana Cooper. She and her husband Antony Beevor, author of *Inside the British Army* and *Crete: The Battle and the Resistance*, live in London with their daughter Nella.

ARTEMIS COOPER

WATCHING IN THE DARK

A CHILD'S FIGHT FOR LIFE

PENGUIN BOOKS

PENGUIN BOOKS

Published by the Penguin Group
Penguin Books Ltd, 27 Wrights Lane, London W8 5TZ, England
Penguin Books USA Inc., 375 Hudson Street, New York, New York 10014, USA
Penguin Books Australia Ltd, Ringwood, Victoria, Australia
Penguin Books Canada Ltd, 10 Alcorn Avenue, Toronto, Ontario, Canada M4V 3B2
Penguin Books (NZ) Ltd, 182–190 Wairau Road, Auckland 10, New Zealand

Penguin Books Ltd, Registered Offices: Harmondsworth, Middlesex, England

First published by John Murray Ltd 1992
Published in Penguin Books 1993
1 3 5 7 9 10 8 6 4 2

Printed in England by Clays Ltd, St Ives plc

*To the doctors and nurses of
the Westminster Children's Hospital,
who brought Nella back to life*

FOREWORD

AMONTH or so after the events described in this book, I was invited to lunch by Rosie Boycott, an old friend who was then deputy editor of *Harpers & Queen* magazine. She wanted to discuss another story, but all I could talk about was Nella's illness and miraculous recovery. Rosie was a good listener: she too has a daughter, and she prompted me to go on. I meant to tell the story briefly, but it turned into an epic. I apologised. 'Not at all,' said Rosie. 'You've kept me absolutely gripped for –' she looked at her watch – 'forty-five minutes. I think you should write it for us.'

At first I was full of misgivings; it was too personal and painful to write. But having discussed it with my husband Antony Beevor, who was very encouraging, I realised I did want to write it down. I could live with the experience better if the story was out on paper, and not still churning around inside me.

Antony's friend and publisher John Murray was very concerned about Nella at the time of the crisis; and soon after publication of the article in *Harpers & Queen*, he urged me to develop the story into a book. I am deeply indebted to his encouragement, enthusiasm and suggestions. Gail Pirkis has been a wonderful editor, whose skill gave me a whole new perspective on the book. I have had invaluable help from staff of the Westminster Children's Hospital, who were key participants in the drama. I am particularly grateful to Amanda Wakefield and Brenda Creany, who were on duty the day Nella was admitted; and Dr Peter Sullivan, who greatly increased my understanding of what happened and the implications of her case for other children in the future.

If Nella had died, I do not think I would have found the strength to write about it; but however harrowing the passage on which I was working, I could always hear her chirping away upstairs, as she played with Clare Brown. Clare was her nanny during the crisis, and is still with us. She made Nella's long days in hospital infinitely brighter with her warmth and companionship.

I have never lived through such a terrible time as the early days of Nella's illness, and I am very grateful to everyone who prayed for her and thought about her. I doubt I could have managed it without the tremendous support of all my family, particularly my mother, Anne Norwich, and my mother-in-law, Kinta Beevor. Kinta was the most stalwart of all, and I shall never forget how generous she was with her time. My father and step-mother, John Julius and Mollie Norwich, were a great comfort in the early days of the crisis, as were my brother Jason, and my sister Allegra who is Nella's godmother. My sister-in-law Sheila Beevor and her daughter Lucy often kept Nella company, and Sheila brought Nella one of the best presents anyone could give to a sick baby in hospital: a shiny, helium-filled balloon. Jamie Fergusson, Nella's godfather, dropped in to see us whenever he could. My aunt Atalanta Clifford was particularly kind in devoting so much time to sit with Nella, for she has spent months of her own life in hospital.

I was even more touched when friends such as Debbie Grossman, Jane Harter and Peggy Carswell gave up evenings to sit with Nella. I am painfully aware that I have not done justice to the immense support of friends and family in the text of this very personal story; but my gratitude is nonetheless heartfelt. I would also like to thank those whose acts of spontaneous generosity meant so much to Antony and me during Nella's illness: particularly John and Sukie Hemming, and James and Caroline Knox.

My very greatest comfort and support, then as now, came from Antony. I have never felt so close to him as I did when we thought our beloved child was dying. I am also deeply grateful for the love, encouragement and effort he has put into this book.

I would like to thank ICI, who so kindly donated the Epidermal Growth Factor (EGF) necessary for Nella's treatment; and Professor Nicholas Wright, the acknowledged expert on the effect of EGF in the gut, who followed and advised on her case. Without any question though, our very greatest thanks are owed to the doctors and nurses of the Westminster Children's Hospital, who never gave up: particularly Dr Martin Brueton, the consultant; Mr Zeid Tabara, the surgeon; Dr Trotty Kirwin, the anaesthetist; and Dr Peter Sullivan, the Lecturer in Child Health. Without their skill and dedication, Nella would not be alive today. They have done more for Antony and me, and for Nella, than we can ever thank them for.

CHAPTER ONE

ANTONY and I married late in life. We were both writers, both rather set in our ways, and we were in no hurry to have children. Sometimes, we had tentative conversations about the future. When we asked each other, 'Do *you* want children?' the answer seemed to be, 'If you do, then I do.'

In the spring of 1989, I was looking forward to the publication of my book *Cairo in the War*, and Antony was well-advanced in an intensive programme of interviews for his next book, an anatomy of the British Army. In early May, he set off for the Falklands.

A few days later, I found out I was pregnant.

I was so happy, yet it still felt so unreal, so strange. Outwardly, nothing had changed – yet inside my body, a human being who would alter my whole life had started to grow. I longed to tell Antony, yet I did not want to spoil it on a crackly line to the Falklands when we were eight thousand miles apart.

I went to collect him very early one morning from RAF Brize Norton in Oxfordshire. He had undergone a seventeen-hour flight from a sub-Antarctic winter with a refuelling stop in the tropical heat of Ascension Island, before landing in England on a fine spring day. After experiencing three seasons in under twenty-four hours, no wonder he looked disorientated. He could not remember which side of the car to get in, and once inside, he slumped in the passenger seat beside me.

I must give him a chance to get his bearings, I thought,

1

before springing this on him. So I hugged the news to myself and asked him about the Falklands. He soon tired of talking.

'Wait till I get the photographs developed,' he said, 'that will make the story much more interesting.'

There was a pause. I thought I had better tell him before he fell asleep; besides, if I held in the news much longer I would burst.

'Guess what?' I said.

'What?'

'I'm pregnant.'

There was a stunned silence as Antony tried to absorb the fact. 'Well, well, well,' he said, shaking his head in bemused delight. He stroked and patted my leg as we drove back to Fulham. 'Well, well, well ... So we're going to be parents. We'll have to grow up now, won't we?'

Because I was, to use that depressing medical term, an 'elderly primagravida', I was strongly urged to have an amniocentesis, a test which checks for certain foetal abnormalities. This means taking a sample of the amniotic fluid that surrounds the baby, and I was not looking forward to it.

My mother Anne came to hold my hand, and I was very grateful for her company.

'Are you going to give me a local anaesthetic?' I asked the specialist.

'No, it's not worth it. The anaesthetic is worse than the real thing.'

I lay down on the couch, the lights were switched off, and we all turned to the television screen. A picture, looking much like a satellite weather report, appeared as the ultrasound probe was moved over my abdomen. Suddenly, I saw the foetus: a head, a perfectly formed spine, spindly arms and legs. It looked like one of those delicate, translucent sea-creatures which, magnified thousands of times, occasionally appear in the *National Geographic*. I saw its heart flutter. Its stomach was a black dot, its brain two cloudy beans within the luminous shell of its skull. It had fingers, feet, knees – and it was moving around in a constant, jerky dance. I had never seen anything so alive, and the sight of it moved me to tears.

The baby's activity filled the womb, and meant that there was no safe place to introduce the needle. I was rather alarmed when the specialist said, 'Well, we'll just have to go in shallow and see what happens.'

I clutched my mother's hand and clenched my teeth; but the sensation of the needle going in could barely be described as pain, and although two samples were taken, it was all over in seconds. Then, as a souvenir, I was given a picture of the baby. I was very happy to have it, but it looked nothing like the dazzling little creature we had been watching – more like a Danish pastry in a snowstorm.

To my enormous relief, the results of the test showed that the baby was normal. I knew that the hospital were also aware of the sex of the child, but I didn't want to know. It would destroy the mystery of this unborn being, who embodied all of our human past, and all my hopes for the future.

I began the research for my next book, but at every opportunity I went up to the room we were preparing at the top of the house. Antony called this the nesting instinct, and every time I went upstairs he would say 'Nesting again, are you?' My mother gave me a beautiful Moses basket, and Antony's mother Kinta set to work knitting bootees, bonnets and cardigans. My sister-in-law, Magdalena, had saved all her daughter's baby clothes, and these were pulled out of tissue paper, washed, and arranged in more tissue paper in drawers upstairs. They looked so tiny, more like doll's clothes.

I bought a small library of books and manuals about

3

pregnancy, childbirth and breast-feeding, and joined ante-natal classes organised by the National Childbirth Trust. I was determined to try and give birth without heavy drugs, and hired a birth-pool: at that time, the West London was the only NHS hospital able to offer such an option.

At first I was prone to bouts of nausea and heartburn, though the sickness came in the evening rather than the morning and was cured by drinking a mixture of plain yogurt and soda water. The sickness faded after three months, and my belly started growing. It was much harder than I had imagined. I felt stirrings, so faint they might have been bubbles of gas – but the first kick was unmistakable. I was sitting in the bath, looking at my belly rising out of the water, when the baby gave such a punch that I was almost knocked sideways, and I saw a momentary bulge which marked the point of impact. Luckily, the baby was not often so violent; but it had a knack of kicking just as I was drifting off to sleep.

During the middle three months of my pregnancy I felt marvellous, though when I was out and about life was an ignominious dash from one loo to the next. In the last three months, the heartburn returned and sleep was badly inter-rupted by the alternating needs to drink and have a pee. It became progressively more difficult to put on socks and tie shoe-laces.

I often thought about the baby, and what sort of a person it would be. For my own sake I fervently hoped that it would have a calm and happy disposition, but I tried not to endow it with any more qualities – after all, it was not even born. Both Antony and I are also rather superstitious. Giving the baby a personality seemed to be tempting fate, and for the same reason we didn't discuss names until the eighth or ninth month. Since Antony hates being called Tony and my name has undergone every variation from Arty to Mouse, we thought carefully about the effect of diminutives. Adam seemed pretty indestructible; and for a girl, we decided on Eleanor, which we would shorten to Nella.

By the time Antony drove me to hospital on 18 January, the contractions were coming every five minutes; but my labour was long, and very slow at first.

'I could give you some pethidine,' said the midwife.

It was three in the morning, and I had been in the delivery room for four hours. However, the contractions were not too unbearable so I said, 'No thanks. I'd rather do this without drugs.'

'Up to you,' said the midwife, 'but a shot of pethidine now will make your labour shorter, and its effect will probably have worn off by the time the baby comes.'

I was convinced, instantly. Like many before me I discovered that the principles of New Age, drug-free motherhood are easily abandoned once labour starts in earnest.

With the help of the birth-pool and gas and air, I managed to cope without any more drugs. Antony was there through every stage – at one point I was hanging from around his neck, trying to push the baby out but it wouldn't budge. Like many men, Antony is very squeamish and looks ill when people describe their operations. Yet he has no trouble coping with the gorier sides of life when they are in front of his eyes.

The baby was finally delivered at three in the afternoon. It was a girl – Nella – perfect in every detail and weighing seven pounds three ounces.

After her birth, I was taken in a wheelchair from the delivery room to the maternity ward, with Nella in my arms. Antony walked beside us. I felt wonderful: very sore, but relaxed and utterly exhausted – like one does after heavy exercise. All I could see of Nella was the top of her head. I tried to kiss it, but it was too far down. She was slumped against me at a funny angle. Her body was very small and floppy, worn out with the effort of being born. I tried to prop her up a little, but my arms felt long and clumsy, like wooden splints. I held her as close as I could, and soon we were lying down, side by side in a clean white bed.

Nella and I spent the next six days in hospital. My only disappointment was that I found breast-feeding too painful to go on with, but Nella thrived on limitless love and Ostermilk.

She was a very easy baby. Her crying was a gentle bleat, more musical – at least to my ears – than some of the fretful wails on the ward. When she had drunk her fill of milk, she fell asleep. I could not keep my eyes off her, as she lay on a fleece in a transparent plastic crib beside my bed. Her hands were remarkably long and tapering, with elegant oval nails; and the fastidious, self-contained expression on her upturned face made her look like an elderly Japanese gentleman.

I enjoyed life on Annie Zunz Ward, which was big enough for twenty-eight women and their babies. At noon, a large West Indian woman in a white overall would call 'Loonch-time, ladies!' and all the new mothers would sit down at a table which ran the length of the room, to build themselves up with solid nursery food like cottage pie and apricot crumble with custard. As we ate, we occasionally cast apprehensive glances over our shoulders.

A few weeks before, there had been a terrible story in the newspapers about a mother and her baby, who had been born in St Thomas's Hospital. A strange woman, posing as a member of the hospital staff, had told the mother she wanted to weigh her baby, and had simply taken it away. Haunted by this story, I never left Nella alone for longer than it took to go to the loo – and then I asked one of the women next to me to keep an eye on her. I took my baths only when I could leave someone in charge. The first time I

6

asked my mother to do sentry duty she said, 'What shall I do if someone comes up and says she's got to be weighed?'

'Pick Nella up and go with them,' I said sternly. 'Just don't let her out of your sight.'

On the sixth day after Nella's birth, Antony arrived to drive us home. He had been so busy getting everything ready for our arrival that he had forgotten to bring my clothes and shoes. Brimming with contrition he offered to go back and get them – but I was so longing to get home I didn't mind. Outside the cold was sharpened by a freezing January wind, and by the time Antony brought the car round to the front it was raining. Clutching Nella in a cocoon of blankets, I walked down the steps with my dressing-gown flapping round my ankles. We must have made a touchingly Dickensian sight, Nella and I – like a disgraced woman and her bastard baby turned out into the storm by heartless employers. Luckily, Antony was waiting at the bottom of the steps with the car door open.

Home looked so bright and fresh and welcoming I nearly cried with the joy of being back, and Antony's mother Kinta had cooked up all sorts of delicacies which looked deliciously light and fresh compared to stodgy hospital food. For the first few weeks, I slept with Nella in the airy white room at the top of the house which we had prepared for her.

Nella was very contented and even-tempered. Her resemblance to an elderly Japanese gentleman faded as her cheeks grew round and fat, and the line of her jaw vanished under plump jowls. Her eyes grew larger and rounder and, to my great delight, they turned a velvety brown with thick, dark lashes: just like Antony's. Her reddish-gold hair was thickest on top, and as it grew it formed a very short fringe on her domed forehead.

I had never imagined I could love her so much; but for someone brought up to believe that free evenings and

7

weekends were basic human rights, motherhood came as a dreadful shock. The incessant, non-stop grind of it made me very irascible – but never when I was with her. Antony bore the brunt of my bad temper, with great patience.

Nella was baptised in March, at the Church of St Mary's, Paddington. Under a fine woollen shawl my mother had bought for the occasion, Nella wore the same robe Antony had been christened in, and her bare arms stuck out of it like pink sausages. A cousin of Antony's brought us some Jordan water in a tonic bottle, and it was quickly decanted into the font. John Foster, an old friend and the vicar of St Mary's, urged us all to keep up with the responses even if Nella started yelling. 'I expect she will,' he added, 'because I haven't had a chance to warm the Jordan water.'

Nella did not yell. Her arms jerked and she gasped as the water trickled down her head. Then she relapsed into wary silence.

Soon after Nella's christening, Clare Brown came to look after her. Slim and pretty, with a quiet, cheerful voice, Clare became very fond of her charge.

'I do hope you don't mind me saying so,' said Clare on one occasion as she was giving Nella her lunch, 'but I think of her as my little sister.' She could not have said anything that would have given me greater pleasure.

With Nella in such capable and loving hands, there was nothing to stop me shutting the door of my room and getting on with my work. Yet I kept the door open, and would listen out for Clare's footsteps on the stairs: I did not want to miss the sight of Nella's bright little face, smiling at me over her shoulder. I would usually desert my word-processor and follow them into the kitchen, to spend a happy half-hour in their company.

Nella was irresistible, it was like being in love. I couldn't go long without wanting to hold and kiss her. The warm folds of her neck smelled sweet and fresh, and I loved listening to the gentle snuffly noises she made when her head was next to mine. Bath-time was a delight. Nella was always happy in water, yet my favourite moment was when I lifted her out of the bath and wrapped her in a warm towel, and cuddled her on my lap. After her bath we had another full half-hour of uninterrupted love, as I read her a story and gave her a bottle of milk. She rarely protested about going to bed, but if she was wakeful I would sing. She would become very still and I would feel her whole body listening, as she looked at me with clear, open eyes.

If Nella cried, it was usually because she was overtired. She was not prone to 'colic' or stomach upsets, and her appetite was excellent. I don't think she had any teeth when she ate her first peach. I held the fruit and she buried her face in it, making voluptuous slurping noises, with a look of total concentration in her eyes.

I saw Nella with such extraordinary clarity that I could almost feel the peachy texture of her skin, and the soft hairs of her eyebrows. The best time to watch her was when she was looking at a book. Her hands, so pudgy and childish, moved in a surprisingly deft and adult way as she turned the pages – she never tore them deliberately. She looked at the pictures in silence, her unclouded, uncluttered mind utterly absorbed; but I had only to shift position a little and she'd drop the book at once, grin at me and hold out her stubby arms to be picked up. Her arms were still so short, she could not touch the top of her head.

Before her arrival, I had always preferred small animals to babies. Now, almost every young animal I saw on television or in magazines looked astonishingly like Nella. It was that look of solemn innocence that seemed so heart-breakingly precious and vulnerable.

We have never taken so many photographs as we did in those early months. Antony wondered whether all those flash-bulbs might be damaging her eyes, but Nella didn't mind them, she enjoyed being photographed. Every moment of her babyhood seemed worthy of record, especially when she was wearing her Mrs-Bridges-style sunhat, which made her look like a very expensive pot of jam. She would sit in her chair, happily sucking teething rings or her clothes. She laughed and babbled at Antony and me and Clare, and her grandmothers, but with strangers she was alert and watchful.

One weekend, when we were staying with Antony's mother in Kent, Kinta suggested (very gently) that Nella might be a bit fat. I disagreed hotly – but Kinta had far more experience of babies than I had, so I fretted about Nella's jowls and kept looking at them from different angles. I could not deny she was well-covered. However, Kinta amply made up for her remark as she said goodbye to us on Sunday afternoon. She kissed Nella, who was cooing and chortling in my arms.

'Do you know,' she said, 'I really think she is the happiest baby I have ever seen.' Seven days later, the nightmare began.

CHAPTER TWO

I HAD always heard that babies can fall ill very rapidly, but Nella had never been unwell in all the eight months of her life. When I heard other mothers complaining of the coughs and colds and ear infections of their offspring I thought of my robust child with quiet satisfaction. So I was quite unprepared when, on the first weekend in September, she went from perfect health to the brink of death in twenty-four hours.

It started in the early hours of Sunday morning, with several bouts of violent retching. Then came stomach cramps, which were brief and terrifying. While they lasted she jerked in my arms and screamed with pain. By four o'clock they had subsided, and she fell into an exhausted sleep.

Nella woke late, evidently feeling better. She drank some milk and the horrors of the night shrank away as I spooned sloppy Weetabix into her mouth. A couple of hours later she sicked it all up and the retching started again, though less violently. Antony got on his bicycle and raced off to the Earl's Court Road, where there was a 24-hour chemist. We tried to give her some water with the glucose, salt and vitamin mixture he had brought back, but she could not keep that down either.

We called the doctor who came as soon as he could – at about three in the afternoon. He asked us a great many questions, and seemed reassured when I told him she had had no diarrhoea. This had already eased my anxiety for a health visitor once told me, 'It's all right if they're sick, and it's all right if they have diarrhoea; it's when they get the two together that you need to start worrying.'

The doctor adjusted his stethoscope and gave Nella a thorough examination. She objected strongly to the wooden spatula against her tongue as he examined her throat, but she was quite calm as he pressed and felt his way round her abdomen. He diagnosed a tummy bug.

'You'll see a lot of this sort of thing, as she grows up,' he said ruefully. Then he wrote out a prescription. 'Retching in babies can become spasmodic,' he explained. 'Once they start they can't stop. This ought to sort it out. If it still hasn't worked after two or three hours, repeat the dose.'

The medicine did seem to work and she was calm and dopey for a few hours, but that evening the retching recommenced. We gave her another dose of the medicine, and again it calmed her, but not for long.

We were up with her virtually all night, in the half-darkness of her room, which was lit only by the light on the landing. She doubled up with pain when the spasms of dry retching came, but it was not the screaming pain of the night before. The spasms would subside, leaving Nella so exhausted that she was asleep almost before they were over. She wouldn't take any water. We would put her gently back in her cot, hoping that the spasm just over was the last, but it wasn't. Within twenty minutes – less as the night wore on – the cycle started again. We took it in turns to pick her up, hold her and croon to her as the spasms waxed and waned, and then lay her down again. It was our second night with almost no sleep, and we both felt light-headed and mechanical.

At about five o'clock on Monday morning Nella vomited a dark brown, viscous fluid. I mopped it up with a muslin square, and carried her into the bathroom to change her nappy. I turned on the light and laid her down on the changing table, and saw with horror just how ill she looked. Her body was limp, the skin yellowish-grey, her eyes huge and hooded and much darker than usual. I snapped out of my zombie-like state and asked Antony to change her nappy while I went to telephone the doctor again.

At that time in the morning there was only an answering service. I explained that I needed to speak to a doctor urgently. An indifferent female voice told me that that was impossible, both doctors were out on call. I was about to argue with her when I heard Antony shout, 'Don't bother with the doctor! There's blood in her nappy. We'll take her straight to hospital.'

I raced upstairs. The nappy was dry except for a little stain of blood the size of a finger-nail. I agreed that the time had come to take her to Casualty.

Clare slept in the room next to Nella's; and although she did not look after her at night, she had not had much sleep either. We were both trembling as she helped me get things together and I dressed Nella: her eyes were half-closed, and she was weak and floppy like a new-born baby. Antony went to get the car. Luckily, I had the presence of mind to take the stained muslin square and the blood-stained nappy with me.

All the tiredness of the night vanished in the cool dawn air, damp with the first hint of autumn. I held Nella close, wrapped in a shawl. Even the whimpering had stopped, for she was barely conscious. Antony drove quickly and smoothly. The streets were deserted, and only the traffic lights maintained a sign of life.

At the Charing Cross Hospital, I hurried down long corridors with my inert bundle, following the signs to Casualty. I heard Antony's footsteps behind me as he ran to catch up after parking the car. The hospital appeared as deserted as the streets outside. Not even the cleaners had arrived. To my relief, we were alone in the reception area;

13

but the receptionist, unimpressed by our controlled desperation, took down our particulars with maddening deliberation.

Time was hard to judge, but everything seemed to be taking far too long. A young woman doctor came and listened to our story, then looked uncertainly at the stained muslin and the nappy. She gave us a bottle of glucose water and went away again. Nella was disturbingly passive. She had no strength left even to support her head, and from the colour of her skin and the dullness of her eyes, it seemed as if her life was draining away in front of us. We thought we had been abandoned, but in fact the doctor had gone to organise an abdominal X-ray.

The X-ray revealed an intussusception – a blockage caused by a section of intestine rolling up on itself like the finger of a rubber glove. Nella was admitted, and we were escorted to the children's ward on the first floor.

The most immediate concern was to get some fluid into her – intravenously. A fat, motherly nurse held Nella in her arms. I knelt on the floor and stroked her head, and beside me an inexperienced doctor probed unsuccessfully for veins in her wrists. The veins of a baby are very small and concealed in surface fat, so finding one can be very difficult. Again and again she stuck the needle in with trembling hands. Nella, too weak to cry, whimpered with pain and fear. Then the ward sister came in, a woman with neat grey curls and a competent expression. To my relief, she firmly suggested that another doctor might have better luck; and the novice, no doubt equally relieved, took herself off.

Nella was moved into a glass-fronted cubicle. 'We've got to set up some drips,' said the sister. 'I don't think you'd better watch.'

We were shown into the cubicle next door. I listened out for Nella, but all I could hear were multiplying footsteps on the linoleum as a team of doctors and nurses gathered round the bed, tense voices, and the squeaky wheels of trolleys bringing in batteries of equipment. A young Asian doctor appeared from Nella's cubicle. He had a striped shirt and a plump, good-looking face. He went to the telephone and began a series of calls, during which he had his back to us. I could not hear what he said, but the serious tone of his voice conveyed urgency.

Roles had been reversed. When we had arrived in Casualty, it had taken some time to alert the hospital staff to the fact that Nella was in mortal danger. But now that they were alerted they seemed to be over-reacting: we were the ones who could not accept how bad things were, or how redundant we felt. Nella had been taken out of our arms, and into an alien world over which we had no control.

I walked up and down a bit of corridor leading to some empty consulting rooms. The walls were decorated with childish paintings and posters. One of these showed a woodland hospital, where pixies treated squirrels and mice for cuts, colds and minor fractures. I looked at it with both irritation and longing. The image was as bright and sugary as a lollipop, and yet how cosy and familiar it looked compared to the harsh reality we had been pitched into. How long would we be here? When could we go home? I imagined us going home alone, without her, and the thought was unbearable. My stomach and chest felt tense. From time to time I took quick, deep breaths, hoping to ease the tension, but it didn't work. My rising fear produced a taste in my mouth so bitter, that even scalding hospital tea could not wash it away.

Antony went downstairs to get the parking meter change from the car to telephone our parents.

'We've arranged for a transfer,' the ward sister told us when he returned.

'Why?' I asked. The Charing Cross seemed so enormous, I could not imagine they had no room for Nella.

'She needs surgery, and we have no paediatric surgery unit here. There's a bed waiting for her at the Westminster Children's Hospital.' With an encouraging smile, she handed me Nella's clothes. 'Good luck.'

Nella was now dressed in a white ward gown several sizes too big. The procession that set off towards the ambulance also seemed out of all proportion to her body, which barely took up a quarter of the stretcher. Besides myself there were two porters, a nurse, and the doctor we had seen on the telephone, who was holding a large syringe on a timer pump which was attached to Nella's wrist. The stretcher was strapped into place in the ambulance and I sat beside her, with the doctor and nurse opposite.

'How fast do you want me to go?' the driver asked the doctor, before closing the rear doors.

'Not too fast, I don't want her shaken around. We've got enough in the syringe for thirty minutes.'

'It'll take more like forty, this hour of the morning.' The rush-hour had already started in the world outside.

'Thirty-five?'

'OK, thirty-five.'

The ambulance set off briskly. I was glad that they didn't turn the siren on, for Nella might have been very distressed by the noise and the lurching about. Her eyes were open and unfocused, but she did turn her head from time to time, and sometimes she looked at me. I thought she was drifting in and out of consciousness. Was she in any pain? The doctor said she was probably too dazed to feel much. I was pretty dazed too. Tiredness, fear, and the sheer disbelief that this could be happening to us gave everything a dream-like quality. Nella turned her head again, and more of that dark brown, viscous liquid trickled out of her mouth. I later learnt that it was a mixture of bile and blood.

We made it to the Westminster Children's Hospital in exactly thirty-five minutes. All I saw of the hospital was a high brick wall with a concrete ramp going up to a heavy door – like a prison, I thought. Once inside, we were in what appeared to be a kindergarten – in fact, the out-patients hall. I saw little tables and chairs, toys, mobiles, a rocking-horse – all the trappings of childhood that Nella might not live to see. It looked rather empty, but a few people glanced curiously at the stretcher and our little procession as we walked the length of a huge, brightly coloured frieze depicting the animals leaving the Ark.

We squeezed into the deep hospital lift and went up to Nathan Ward on the third floor. At the end of its long corridor hung with posters of cheerful babies was the intensive care unit. Nella was wheeled straight in and out of sight. Parting from her was a wrench, yet at the same time I felt a profound relief not to have to look at her pinched little face, her huge dark eyes gazing blankly up at me. She was someone else's responsibility now.

A low-voiced sister called Wendy took my arm and led me to a room for parents at the opposite end of the corridor. The room was at tree-top height; through the plane trees, I could see the Westminster School playing-fields. Antony arrived. He had been waiting downstairs all this time, having driven from the Charing Cross with needless haste.

CHAPTER THREE

I T was not hard to guess how bad things were. More than once, we were asked whether we wanted to talk to a priest or a psychologist. 'No, thank you,' said Antony firmly. 'We've got each other.' A strange face, no matter how sympathetic, would have been an intrusion.

I longed to rest, but knowing that Nella was hanging between life and death made me feel like a spring wound up so tight that I might snap at any moment. I could not even sit down, let alone stretch out on the bed. Antony and I stood at the window and looked out at the playing-fields, watching the boys of Westminster School shouting and running about. How I envied their parents, who were starting the week secure in the knowledge that their sons were safe and well. The playing-fields emptied, filled again, and emptied. As time passed tiredness began to dull the tension. We waited, taking it in turns with the bed and the armchair. There wasn't much to say. Sometimes we clung to each other. Sometimes we just held hands. It was the first time I had heard Antony weeping.

As the morning wore on and the suspense became unbearable, we went down the corridor to the intensive care unit. I did not dare go in for fear of what I might see; Antony went in first. 'It's all right,' he said. 'Come on.'

About a dozen people stood round the bed. They parted to let us come forward, then carried on with their consultations. Nella lay on a white sheet, an oxygen hood over her head and her body under a network of tubes and electrodes connected to machines with blinking digital displays. I thought she was unconscious, but sometimes her unfocused eyes would open for a minute and then close again.

After the rush of getting her there by ambulance, we thought she would be wheeled into the operating theatre immediately, so that the bit of gut which had turned in on itself could be straightened out as quickly as possible. But operations on babies are not done without much preparation, and they had to make sure that her heart, lungs and blood pressure were stable enough for her to withstand the anaesthetic.

Suddenly an alarm started bleeping. The doctors and nurses went into emergency action and Antony pulled me away: he did not want me to see what was happening. Nella had collapsed, and he had caught a glimpse of her face. The image later gave him nightmares.

Antony's telephone calls brought my mother Anne up from Sussex, and his mother Kinta from Kent. By late morning they were both with us. I had felt an urgent need to see my mother, and as soon as I was in her arms I felt stronger. She had brought some sandwiches, and Kinta made us some tea. I could not eat much; my stomach felt as if it was knotted into a hard ball.

The doctors managed to stabilise Nella, and she was wheeled down to the operating theatre at around noon. After an hour or so we had some news: she was in the recovery room downstairs, and was in a stable condition. The word 'stable' sounded reassuringly solid and the tension loosened a little.

Not long afterwards Dr Martin Brueton, the consultant, came to see us. He looked extremely serious, and I felt the fear build up again inside me. He told us that when the surgeon opened her up, the only sign of the inverted intestine was an inflamed mark. The shock of surgery may have been enough for the folded stretch to unravel itself.

However, the state of the small intestine (the one which looks like a plate of spaghetti, as opposed to the large intestine which looks like an exhaust pipe) was critical. It looked as though she had picked up a very severe form of gastro-enteritis. Had we just come back from Asia, or Africa perhaps? We assured him that we had not travelled that far since our honeymoon in India, four years before.

'Well, we'll see what happens,' said Dr Brueton. 'She's holding her own well enough at the moment.'

Since there seemed to be a lull in developments, Antony, Kinta and I decided to go home while Anne stayed in the Parents Room. She promised to ring if anything happened. We were desperately tired, longing for a bath, and I thought I had better collect some things for the night.

Before leaving we went to see Nella. While she was in surgery they had installed two lines in her neck: one for the blood products, and one for drugs. They were held in place with adhesive tape and stitched to the skin. They looked very uncomfortable, and I was glad she was unconscious. Since the possibility of infection in her gut was very high (though it was not yet confirmed), she was given antibiotics. She looked red and puffy, and yellow mucus was drying round her nose and lips. I kissed the soft hair on top of her head, and left for Fulham.

Clare, who had been waiting nervously for news, met us at the front door. We tried to explain the situation as calmly and rationally as we could. I had been in the hospital for so many hours that Nella's present condition seemed an improvement; but to Clare, who had never imagined that the situation was so desperate that Nella would need an operation, the news was devastating. The horrified look on her face heightened my own anxiety; though by now I was so tired that not even anxiety could remain intense for long.

Since Nella was obviously going to remain in hospital for the forseeable future, we suggested to Clare that she might like to go back to her family in Hastings, and we would keep her informed of developments. Clare took the train home in a daze. It was not until she started telling her parents about what had happened to Nella that the reality sank in, though even then it seemed unbelievable: she kept comparing Nella's face as it had been on Friday, laughing and rosy, with the exhausted, sallow baby she had last seen at five o'clock that morning.

To Antony and me the situation began to look better from home than it had in hospital, despite its shattering effect on Clare. So far we had been told very little; and with our ignorance of medicine and our confidence in the doctors, we began to imagine that she was not as ill as she had seemed in the hospital. My father John Julius rang while I was in the bath. He had called just before Nella's operation, and wanted to know how things had gone. When answering, Antony sounded worried, but not unduly so. The operation had sorted out the blockage in her gut, so now that was gone the infection should soon fade away and everything would be all right. Much relieved, John Julius said he would call again in the morning. Neither Antony on the telephone, nor I, relaxing at last in a hot bath, had any idea that Nella's condition had taken a serious turn for the worse.

Amanda had come on duty at 12.30: this was about an hour before we went home, while Nella was still on the operating table. As the sister in charge, Amanda would be heading the nursing team on Nathan Ward for the next nine hours – and it did not look as if it was going to be an easy shift.

Due to a severe staff shortage, she was the only RSCN – Registered Sick Children's Nurse – on duty. The rest were qualified nurses, but had not finished their full paediatric training. The most promising of them had an Irish lilt in her voice which always rose at the end of a sentence, reflecting a natural cheerfulness. Her name was Brenda, and she was due to take her exams in a week's time.

Amanda was briefed on Nella's condition by the outgoing sister: she would be coming up to the ward from theatre soon, and no problems were anticipated – Nella would probably need no more than the usual post-operative care. Her bed was prepared in the intensive care room, and a ventilator was made ready. Barring unforeseen complications, Amanda expected Nella to be in a room on the corridor by nightfall. She put Brenda in charge of the newcomer, leaving her free to keep an eye on the two premature, ventilated babies who needed constant attention. The situation was not ideal. There should have been at least two RSCNs on Nathan Ward, preferably with intensive care experience as well. Amanda had tried to find another at the last moment, but none was available.

Nella came back from surgery shortly after one o'clock. She was accompanied not only by the anaesthetist and some nurses, but also by the surgeon, Mr Zeid Tabara, which was very unusual as Nella seemed to be in a stable condition. Nella did not need a ventilator, though a tube blowing air and oxygen was placed near her head.

At about three o'clock, Nella's condition started to deteriorate. She began to lose a considerable amount of fluid from her rectum, and she was also vomiting. The fluid in her stomach had to be aspirated. Her blood pressure dropped. The doctor in charge now began pumping blood products into her. At one point there was an anxious call from Haematology: was the doctor aware of the sheer quantity of valuable blood products that were being poured into this child? The doctor knew very well, but he had to keep up the level of fluid in her body in order to maintain her blood pressure: when this falls below a certain level, there is a grave danger of kidney failure and loss of blood to the brain.

I felt quite calm as we drove back to Vincent Square late that afternoon; but as soon as I breathed in that faint hospital smell of floor polish and surgical spirit, I was overwhelmed by alarm and uncertainty. We went up to the third floor in silence, gazing at the yellow oxygen cylinder on wheels which stood in the corner marked PLEASE DO NOT REMOVE THE OXYGEN CYLINDER FROM THIS LIFT UNDER ANY CIRCUMSTANCES. I walked fast up the long corridor of Nathan Ward, but the dread of what might have happened to Nella while we had been gone made me stop at the doors to the intensive care unit. Once again Antony went in first. I watched him take a step or two into the room and look towards Nella's cot. His expression did not undergo any dramatic change, and from this I understood that she was still there. The moment of relief was short. The faces around the bed looked tense and I did not need to be a doctor to see that her condition had become very serious.

She no longer looked like my child. Her face was dark red, which made her lashes look much paler than usual. Her body was horribly swollen and a large dressing hid the scar of surgery. Her hair was dull and matted, there was dried blood on the bandages around her hands and under her finger-nails. Pale brown patches of blood and fluid stained the sheet on which she lay.

She looked unconscious – but many months later, Amanda revealed that she was more aware of what was going on than I had thought. Although desperately ill, Nella had often opened her eyes. At that stage, she was not being given any sedatives or pain-killers for fear they might adversely affect her blood pressure. I was appalled to hear that Nella had retained any awareness, however dim; but Amanda told me that it was encouraging at the time, for it implied that she had not suffered from lack of oxygen to the brain while her blood pressure was so perilously low.

Antony asked questions. I tried to keep my eyes on Nella but the reality of her was too painful. I turned away, breathing hard, tears in my eyes.

We walked back to the Parents Room in silence, accompanied by Amanda. I felt as though my whole body was made of lead, and could barely move under the crushing weight of one thought: Nella was going to die. Amanda told me later that it had never taken her so much time to walk down that long corridor.

For everyone around Nella's bedside, the most frightening thing about that afternoon was that none of them knew what was wrong with her – they could only react to developments. Results were coming up from the labs all the time and fresh blood samples were going down: an arterial line had been put into her arm, so that blood could be drawn off at regular intervals. The medical staff adjusted what they were doing according to the results; but for the most part they were just trying to keep her hydrated and maintain her blood pressure. Amanda and Brenda worked every minute of that day, without a break. At about eight o'clock, Brenda heard Amanda asking 'Have you had a cup of coffee yet?' There had been no time for coffee, and the pressure did not let up.

Amanda was about to set up the ventilator when the situation became critical. Nella went into shock and despite all the blood fluids being pumped into her, her blood pressure sank alarmingly. They had to find out why she was losing so much fluid. The surgeon, Mr Tabara, thought that the gut might have perforated and the doctors decided that her only chance was another operation. Yet in their hearts, many of those who had witnessed Nella's rapid decline over the past few hours felt that she would never survive another bout of major surgery.

Dr Brueton, Mr Tabara and Amanda walked down to the Parents Room.

'I'm afraid we have to perform another operation,' said

Dr Brueton. 'We don't want to, but there is really no choice.' He explained the situation, and Antony went to sign the consent form. He felt it was tantamount to signing a death warrant, for he was given to understand that her chances were very slim indeed.

From the end of the corridor I watched Nella being wheeled into the lift – I could not bring myself to come any closer. Then we went outside and walked slowly round Vincent Square. Kinta and Anne walked together. Antony and I went ahead, arm in arm, talking about Nella in the past tense. It was not just a case of what Antony calls 'pre-emptive pessimism': it seemed the only way to prepare ourselves for the shock of her death. Nothing, we told ourselves, could take away the last eight months, and her short life had been happy; but this was little comfort as I imagined the desolation of the weeks ahead. I wondered whether that glimpse of a bump under a white sheet on a trolley was my last sight of Nella alive. I saw myself packing up her clothes, her toys.

It was a fine night and we felt better outside than in the Parents Room; but we would hear no news of Nella in Vincent Square, so we made our way back. News came sooner than expected. At about nine-thirty a young nurse came in. She smiled encouragingly and said, 'She's recovering from the operation, and is in a stable condition.' This is a standard way of saying 'The patient is alive and so far there don't seem to be any complications.' Did she add something else, like 'It seems to have gone all right'? I cannot remember for sure; but whatever she said, we understood that the operation had been a success. I felt a great weight slipping away, and we all hugged each other with profound relief.

Our newly lifted hopes were about to be crushed yet again. Soon after the nurse left the room we were visited by Mr Tabara. He had taken off his gown, but he was still wearing surgery clothes – a pale blue tunic, trousers and cap. He sat down and I braced myself, as I always did when one of the doctors appeared. I could feel my shoulders tensing as apprehension drew the knot inside me tighter. Mr Tabara looked very grave. He explained that although no part of the gut was actually perforated or dead, it was extremely damaged – but he had decided not to cut anything.

At the time, I did not realise what a brave decision this was. When Mr Tabara opened Nella up, her gut looked even worse than it had a few hours before. The textbooks say that gut which has undergone such massive damage must be cut out. Yet so much would have had to be removed that Mr Tabara doubted she would survive the operation – they were having difficulty keeping her stable as it was. There was very little time, and he had no senior doctor to confer with – a surgeon in the operating theatre is in sole control, and has to take his decisions alone. He decided to leave things as they were, and closed her up.

Mr Tabara told us that Nella had not been long under the anaesthetic when she had suffered another collapse on the operating table from which they had only just managed to save her. His dark, tired eyes were full of sadness but they did not flinch, and his Arab accent gave the words great precision. 'I'm afraid there is very little hope,' he said.

Now the real waiting began. When I wasn't sobbing, I tried not to think. I looked at the corky texture of the ceiling tiles, and at the flimsy curtains adorned with blob-on-stalk trees and mauve sheep, and tried to avoid the one image that was haunting me: Nella in Antony's arms, as he walked her up and down her room in the early hours of that morning. I could see her exhausted head on his shoulder, the pale shape of her rapidly weakening body in its pink pyjama suit. *Why* hadn't we seen how serious it was then, why hadn't we taken her into hospital a few hours earlier? Would it have made any difference?

All the love I had for Nella, and all the anguish and guilt I was going through, were concentrated into that image of her in Antony's arms. I found it unbearable, yet every train of thought led back to it. When I drifted into a doze, the image sprang out at me with such painful intensity that I called her name aloud, and shook my head like a dog in an attempt to escape from it.

Antony tried to comfort me. He said that we had both been much too tired to think straight that night; and that if we had taken her in any earlier, before the blood appeared in her nappy, we might have been sent home from Casualty without an X-ray which would only have wasted more time. However, he was going through exactly the same agonies of guilt and self-reproach as I was. We tried to convince ourselves that there was no point in chewing over the past and that we had done all we could – but the questions and the remorse kept coming back, no matter how hard one tried to push them away. We took it in turns to lie on the bed. At one point we lay together and dozed, though even when dozing I was on guard for the dreaded image prowling on the edge of consciousness.

Anne and Kinta's reactions were very different. Kinta sat beside the round pine table in the corner, knitting a little blue cardigan for Nella, willing her to live with every stitch. But while Kinta believed in hoping for the best, Anne believed in preparing for the worst. She held my hand and talked softly, saying that I had done everything I could for Nella, but I must accept that she had her own little destiny in which I had no part. I took strength from them both. I have never admired Kinta so much as I did that night, as she knitted away in silent determination; but my mother's words brought comfort. In anguish one sobs, trying to relieve the pent-up emotion building up inside. Effective comforting brings release and warm, free-flowing tears.

Most of the time we waited in silence. Outside our room the corridor was alive with doors opening and closing, trailing babbles of conversation, greetings and bursts of laughter – the ordinary noises of hospital life. Every time I heard a slightly heavier or slower footstep coming in our direction, I expected the doctor whose painful duty it would be to tell us that Nella was dead. I became more and more irritable as the suspense mounted, and the thought that the doctors might be keeping her alive unnecessarily filled me with rage – but I kept my anger to myself. I felt it was something bad, and that if I showed it, Nella really would be snatched away from me.

Instead I begged Antony to ask the doctors to stop fighting to save her, and end the ordeal for that poor bruised little body. I also asked him to stay with her, so that one of us should be near when she died.

Antony approached one of the doctors in the corridor. His voice was breaking up so badly that he had to repeat himself: 'If there really is absolutely no hope . . . please don't keep her alive artificially.'

'We note what you say,' said the young doctor gravely. The perfectly correct response. Perhaps this phrase is taught in the course of medical training: it sounded as if it had been formulated by a lawyer for such occasions.

Antony sat in the intensive care room, opposite the end of Nella's bed, for the rest of the night. Anne and the doctors advised him to leave, saying that he was inflicting needless pain on himself, but he would not budge. I should have been there too but the sight of her was still too painful to bear, so I lay on the bed in the Parents Room and tried not to think. Kinta gave Anne a lift home at three in the morning.

I awoke around dawn, and walked up the corridor to the intensive care room. As I walked I thought, surely I would have been told if she had died? But perhaps the doctors had said no, let her sleep, we'll give her the bad news when she wakes up. As I approached I imagined what I would see: an empty space, an iron cot with a clean sheet smoothed over it.

The first thing I saw was Antony slumped in a chair. Nella was still there, and still alive.

She no longer looked like a human child to me – she had moved on to some other plane. Her face looked still and remote like an effigy, and her body was unrecognisable. Her abdomen, a chocolate-purple colour, was so shiny and distended that it looked like a bladder about to burst. She was so swollen that the nurses could hardly move her – even her joints were almost immobile – though she had to be moved from time to time to avoid pressure sores. The fluids being pumped into her had been reduced since the day before; but although all her tissues were saturated with water, her blood pressure was still low. Blood products were still being dripped into the neck-line to maintain her blood pressure. Her breathing was now controlled by a ventilator: a contraption like a miner's lamp was strapped to her head with a broad bandage to hold the air tube in place. The air tube itself vanished down one nostril into her lungs.

I later learnt that she had struggled hard against the ventilator which, once in position, takes over the patient's breathing. I imagined the mounting pain and horror she must have felt as she choked on the tube being pushed inexorably down her nose, then her throat; the panic as her lungs filled with air she had not inhaled, while she struggled to regain control of that most basic reflex in the body.

Nella was given a muscle relaxant and a pain-killer cum sedative to help her through the ordeal, which was supervised by the anaesthetist, Dr Trotty Kirwin. Both Trotty and Amanda were surprised at the level of sedative Nella had to be given before she calmed down. They hated to see her in such distress, and for her own safety she was sedated as quickly as possible: if the patient resists the ventilator too long there is a danger of the lungs bursting. I was assured that once the ventilator was in place, her illness and heavy sedation would have kept her in some twilight state of consciousness, a long way from what was going on.

As no one knew what had caused Nella's illness, and as her condition was so serious, the doctors took unprecedented risks. They later explained that there was nothing to lose. Nella was given massive doses of immunoglobulins, and a highly potent antibiotic to fight toxins apparently as lethal as those from typhoid. Ceaseless blood transfusions were necessary, for she was bleeding profusely through the walls of her intestine.

Even more serious was the damage done to the lining of the gut, the part which absorbs food: without it, the gut cannot function. Any bad infection in this area would cause some damage; but the lining of Nella's gut had been so saturated with toxins that her body's defence mechanisms had sloughed it altogether.

Yet the doctors had not listened to our plea that if there really was no hope, she should be allowed to die.

In the course of twenty-four hours, Nella had lost so much fluid that they had had to give her the equivalent of six complete blood transfusions. She had gone into shock, she had been brought round twice from a state of collapse, and had withstood two operations. In the course of the night, she underwent a series of crises. The doctors were obliged to use a drug to stimulate her heart, and another to stimulate her kidneys, though they were always aware of the dangers of 'the doctor's disease', the point at which medical intervention begins to cause more problems than the original illness. Every member of the medical, surgical, and nursing teams had worked very hard for her life, and they had refused to give up. As Dr Brueton put it, 'With babies we carry on fighting, even after we've given up hope – and it's amazing how often they surprise you.'

CHAPTER FOUR

I REMEMBER very little about Tuesday, which was a day of watching and waiting. My father rang early, and from his last call to Antony the previous afternoon he expected encouraging news. He was horrified to hear about the night's developments and came round immediately on his bicycle. His cheeks were cold and I could smell the fresh morning air as I clung to him, and he kept saying 'my darling, my darling'.

My step-mother Mollie, my brother Jason and sister Allegra all appeared at various times that morning. I hugged each one for a long time, taking strength not only from their warmth and closeness, but also from their shocked, drawn faces which revealed the extent of their concern for Nella. Allegra met Antony in the corridor. He had come from the intensive care room where he had been sitting with Nella, and when she hugged him he collapsed in tears on her neck.

I was still haunted by my failure to get Nella to hospital sooner, and I was also racked by a guilty secret that I had not dared mention even to Antony. Nella's last proper meal was supper on Saturday evening. It had consisted of home-made chicken broth, thickened with semolina. The semolina was well past its sell-by date, but it looked and tasted all right. I remember thinking that if I boiled it a bit longer than usual it couldn't do her any harm. Two days later, giving Nella the semolina had grown into a crime of monstrous proportions. From the moment she was born I had wanted to protect Nella from every harm; yet now I had

31

to face the fact that I might have poisoned her, perhaps fatally. I could not bear telling Antony, but I resolved to tell the doctors: if I did not, my guilt would be compounded by failure to turn in what could be important evidence.

The medical team on Nella's case consisted of twelve doctors of differing levels of experience, headed by Dr Brueton. They had a meeting every morning around Nella's bedside, which they understandably liked to hold in private. That morning, before leaving the room, I told them about her last meal as calmly as I could. My fears were dismissed at once. It takes more than old semolina to bring a healthy baby to the brink of death.

Perhaps they were only trying to reassure me, for they had no clues as to where she might have picked up this deadly combination of bugs. It could have come from her food, but equally well from the air, the swimming-pool or the swings in the park. Babies between six and twelve months are very vulnerable, because the antibodies inherited from their mothers start to wear off before their own immune systems are fully functional. A number of samples were taken from Nella during that first day but as she was being pumped full of powerful drugs at the same time, the tests were inconclusive.

As I watched the doctors around Nella's bed I thought how unprepared Western mothers are for the death of their children, and what tremendous efforts are made to save them. In our great-grandmothers' generation, a woman could almost count on losing one or more of her children; in some developing countries, only half the children born survive beyond the age of five.

Four years before, in the Aïr Mountains of Niger, I had witnessed a scene which I went over and over again in my mind. I had crossed the Sahara with a group of four friends, of whom I was the only woman. One day, our two Land

Rovers stopped at a village called Mekeli.

A girl of about fourteen came up to me, as stern and commanding as a queen. She spoke in French.

'Do you have medicine?'

'Some, yes . . .'

'Come with me.'

She took me by the hand and led me to a hut, which was made of large mats of plaited straw folded round a wooden frame. She lifted one of the mats and, bending almost double, I entered. It was very dark inside, and stank of unwashed clothes and rancid butter. A young woman sat next to a pile of greasy, indigo-blue cloth. She lifted a corner of the cloth to reveal two tiny babies only a few days old. Their limbs were like twigs, their ribs stuck out, their stomachs were distended. Although the mother had given them nothing but her own milk, they could not keep it down. Very gently she turned the nearest baby's head towards me. Its jaw, angular as an insect's, slowly dropped and it let out a thin, protesting wail; then its eyelids fluttered and it relapsed into silence.

I had a medicine chest full of eye-ointment, aspirin, even antibiotics – but it contained nothing which would have helped. She accepted this in silence, and drew the wrap back over her dying babies.

I found out that Dr Brueton had worked in Africa, and I once asked him if there was anything I could have done.

'No, nothing at all; from what you tell me it sounds as if they had pyloric stenosis, which can only be corrected by surgery. You felt bad because you didn't know what to do, but imagine what it's like being a doctor in that kind of situation; to know exactly what needs to be done, and be unable to do it because there's no hospital, no facilities.'

Both Antony and I felt very strongly that there should be someone with Nella all the time, at least during the day. I knew she was unconscious, but perhaps there was a part of her that could feel the presence of someone who loved her and was willing her to live. When I was with her I would sit by her bed and hold her fingers; sometimes I would lean over and stroke her hair, and talk softly about how brave she was and how much we all loved her. Yet the sight of Nella was still intensely painful. On Tuesday, the second day in hospital, Antony and Kinta sat with her most of the time.

It was not until Wednesday that I could with any calmness look at Nella with drip-needles in her hands and tubes in her nose. I came into the intensive care unit at seven in the morning (Antony had gone home to sleep, for the single bed in the Parents Room was too narrow for us both). It seemed very quiet and peaceful. A doctor was writing up notes in a pool of light at the desk, and Brenda – who had looked after Nella all night – was filling in charts and preparing for the 7.30 hand-over, when the day-shift came on duty. She smiled as I came in, and asked if I had managed to get any sleep.

Nella lay quite still, except for the rise and fall of her ribs as the ventilator pumped them up and down.

'Would you like to swab her mouth with water?' said Brenda. 'It gets so dry.' She showed me where little bottles of sterile water stood on a shelf in the kitchen, and in the drawer of the locker next to Nella's bed were sterile swabs, four to a packet. 'Not too much water, mind . . . That's it.'

According to Brenda, once she had shown me how to perform this little service for Nella I was doing it every five minutes. It made me feel useful at a time when I felt there was so little I could give her, apart from kisses and whispered encouragement.

Later that day, another nurse suggested I might like to clean Nella up a little. At first I was nervous of pulling out a line or jogging an electrode – but as I dabbed away with the dampened balls of cotton wool, her swollen body became more familiar and less disturbing.

I wiped away the dried blood around the bandages on her hands and feet, and wished I could scrape it from under her nails as well. I put vaseline on her dry lips and eyelids. Her lashes were clogged with dried gunk. I kissed the hair on top of her head. My mother had once said that the top of a baby's head has a lovely innocent smell, like ironing boards and digestive biscuits. Nella's now smelt of sweat and bandages, but her hair was the only part of her that remained familiar.

By Wednesday, the quality of waiting had changed. It was less tense. Yesterday, she might have died at any moment. That was still true, but Dr Brueton advised us to try and live one hour at a time. Every hour she lived was an hour gained.

Dr Brueton came to see us twice a day. He was a tall man, rather shy with a fleeting smile, who not only explained things clearly but also gave us time to frame our questions. He had that clean, self-contained quality that many male doctors have; yet beneath his carefully chosen words, his voice was sympathetic.

He told us the infection was still raging in Nella's gut, but she was managing to hold her own. If she survived, she would have to undergo surgery again within the next few days. In the meantime, it was a question of waiting. The longer the operation could be postponed, the easier it would be to tell the difference between those areas of the gut which were going to heal and those which were damaged beyond repair. The latter would have to be cut out.

'Is it possible to live without much gut?' I asked.

'Oh yes. It is possible to live with only a few inches, although life under those conditions is very hard. And the problem is much more complicated in children because they are growing.'

Antony and I had one other question. Nella was still unconscious.

'Is there a possibility of brain damage?'

35

'Yes, there is; but we won't know until she regains consciousness.'

I am a worrier by nature, yet even at the time I was surprised at how calm I was. I could almost feel the defence mechanisms growing in my head like invisible blinkers, to shut out anxiety and speculation. For some reason I did not imagine being the mother of a permanently brain-damaged child and how that would change our lives. Nor did I think of the implications of Nella living with a drastically shortened gut. In that strange limbo between life and death, living hour by hour was easier than I thought it would be.

The awareness that Nella might die became dulled by familiarity, yet I still could not endure the memory of her as she had been the night that the sickness took hold. This image had become a box into which I had crammed all the pain of the last four days: it was dangerously full, but as long as it stayed shut I could keep myself on an even keel. In retrospect I see that this was why I was so calm, though it seemed strange at the time. I had expected to find myself in emotional turmoil; yet although my love for Nella was deeper than ever, I felt cut adrift from all my other feelings, as though they had been amputated and cauterized.

Reality only came in painful flashes. One afternoon, I unfolded the clothes she had worn on the morning we took her to Casualty at the Charing Cross. I had not looked at them since the sister had put them into my hands, just before going downstairs to the ambulance. I picked up the soft blue romper suit, shook it out and gasped – it was split by a jagged rent from top to bottom. Things had been so desperate that morning that Nella's clothes had been ripped away from her, with a pair of sharp hospital scissors.

I wanted everyone to know about what was happening to Nella, so that as many people as possible would be thinking of her and praying for her. My own prayers could not get off the ground, they were so heavy, blunt and self-absorbed: please God, if you're up there, let her live for my sake. What Nella desperately needed were the prayers of other people, prompted only by compassion and addressed to a God they believed in. I had no hesitation in asking for them.

So when I saw a tall figure in a dog-collar in the corridor, I stopped him. I knew that he was Peter Fellows, the hospital chaplain, for a notice in the lift suggested coming to meet him on Fridays at eleven for coffee and a chat. He was young, with a bouncy, upbeat manner. I was told that he had a remarkable rapport with children, and had it not been for the sombre shirt and dog-collar, I could see him presenting a media show for younger viewers on Channel 4. I told him about Nella, and asked him to pray for her.

'Don't worry, I've already started,' he said. 'What's the latest? How did it happen?'

His prayers were no doubt a spontaneous reaction to seeing a child so ill, and I was glad that he had not waited for me to ask for them. From then on I often noticed him in the corridors of the hospital. A few days later I passed him again, when he was obviously in a hurry.

'You are still praying for Nella, aren't you?' I called after him.

'I never stop! They're going up all the time!' he called back.

My sister-in-law Sheila had mentioned the subject of faith-healers when she came to see Nella. I told her I was very keen on the idea, but did not know who to contact. She said she would find out, and the following day she came round with five or six different names and addresses, passed on by friends.

The doctors and nurses were caring for Nella with such skill and dedication that I did not want them disturbed by a dramatic laying-on of hands. I chose a healer in Dorset, who worked long distance and sounded very discreet. I rang her up, and liked her voice at once. She asked me to send her a bit of Nella's hair, which I did. I also sent a photograph of Nella – I thought the healing power would be better directed if she had both.

But if I was superstitious, I was also sceptical. This healer calls her treatment radiesthesia, and it works on a principle resembling that used in water-divining. I did not ask what the treatment actually involved in case the knowledge might destroy my faith in its efficacy.

Kinta had another photograph of Nella, taken at her house in Kent the weekend before she fell ill. Wearing Kinta's gardening hat, she is chuckling and waving at the camera. Kinta wanted to show the photograph to the nurses, but was afraid that I might find it upsetting. On the contrary, I was very pleased she had it with her and we stuck it up above Nella's bed. The nurses were delighted.

'Doesn't she look adorable!' said Brenda. 'Now we know what we're aiming for!'

I too found great comfort in that picture of Nella. Her body lay inert on the bed but, from somewhere else, her spirit was waving to me. Antony, on the other hand, instantly developed a horror of this photograph. He thought the slightly yellow flesh-tone of the print had somehow predicted the illness to come, and he could not bear to look at it.

The doctors hoped to postpone Nella's third operation until Saturday. Her temperature had come down, and the infection was subsiding under the latest onslaught of antibiotics. However, she was using up platelets (cells involved in the blood-clotting process, which are consumed in the presence of infection) at such a rate that they thought some part of the gut might be dead and decaying inside her. The operation was brought forward a day, and scheduled for Friday afternoon.

As is so often the case with air travel and surgery, departure was delayed.

'They're doing some carpentry on a hip at the moment, but it shouldn't be long now,' confided the porter who was due to wheel her down.

The delay made me tense and irritable though I had nothing to do but wait. Ten minutes later, in came Father John Foster, the priest who had baptised Nella. That morning I had left a message on his answering-machine, asking him to pray for her. His response was to come straight round. When I saw his kind, anxious, bespectacled figure hurrying into the room, I was so touched and pleased to see him that I flung my arms round his neck. We talked a little and then he turned to bless Nella, and prayed for her in silence. Soon after, she was wheeled into the lift. Once she was taken away there was still nothing to do except wait, but waiting while someone is having an operation is more focused, more purposeful. One is at last in anticipation of news, and a result.

Of all the doctors we met, none was more reserved and serious than Mr Tabara, the surgeon. However, even Mr Tabara looked a little more hopeful when he came to see us after the operation. He told us that although the whole length of the bowel was very unhealthy, no part was completely dead, and he had not cut out any of it. Instead he had performed an ileostomy, which means cutting the gut and bringing the two cut ends to the surface, so that the doctors could have a better idea of what was going on inside.

Talking to doctors is not like talking to other people. They tell you the truth, but not what they are thinking. Their private thoughts about Nella's condition would probably have plunged me into despair, so it was just as well that I have no telepathic powers. Yet I would scrutinise the faces of Mr Tabara and Dr Brueton as they spoke, waiting for the slightest flicker of the eyes or inflection of the voice that might reveal what lay behind their words.

At one point that day, Dr Brueton had talked of decreasing the support for Nella's blood pressure to see whether she could maintain it herself. That sounded encouraging, but he looked more preoccupied than the last time I had seen him. What had gone wrong? What hasn't he told me? Perhaps he's changed his tone because he thinks my hopes are too high, I thought. Or perhaps he is thinking about another patient. Could it be that he has indigestion? Perhaps he's had a row with his wife.

Sometimes I found I was looking at his face so intently that I hadn't taken in what he said. However, I did manage to grasp the essentials. For the time being, there was no more that surgery could do for Nella. The medical team would keep giving her all the blood products she needed, and they would start to feed her intravenously. There was no telling whether or not the gut would heal – we would just have to wait and see. The best news of all was that, for the present, she was off the danger list. We could think in terms of days, perhaps even weeks, rather than hours.

The knowledge that I no longer had to keep every nerve tense and alert in anticipation of a crisis was a tremendous relief. It seems astonishing in retrospect that I was so insensible to the very real possibility that Nella might yet have to have most of her gut cut out or that she might have suffered brain damage. I was not optimistic about Nella's condition, and although I never visualised what the future might hold, it looked bleak enough; but my mind seemed to be covered in a sort of self-protective Teflon; nothing stuck to it for long.

It was different for Antony, who maintained a better

grasp on reality. On one occasion Dr Brueton said to him, 'You realise, she may never be able to eat solids again.' Unlike myself, he could imagine the life that Nella seemed destined to suffer – tied to an intravenous drip and forced to undergo one operation after another as her body grew. Having been on crutches himself between the ages of three and seven, he knew what it felt like to be a disabled child. It seemed so cruel that Nella, who had fought so hard to survive, should be condemned to such a blighted childhood.

CHAPTER FIVE

O UR life in the hospital was divided between Nella's bedside and the Parents Room. The Parents Room is for mothers who want to stay near a baby in intensive care, and its fittings and furniture were donated by the Friends of the Hospital. It contained a single bed and wash-basin at the far end closest to the window, an armchair, a locker and a small low table with a lamp on it. Nearest the door was a round pine table and four chairs, and an empty bookcase. The carpet was thin and the curtains didn't meet, but it was very comfortable, more like a hotel room than a hospital facility. There was a television on a stand above the bed.

The decoration consisted of a framed Renoir landscape print which I got to know very well, and a small plastic vase into which were stuck a few fly-blown artificial flowers – the sort of thing that stands by an untended grave, and so depressing that I put it away in a drawer.

Normally, both Antony's family and mine are typically Anglo-Saxon. Each of us feels close, but can go quite happily for weeks without seeing one another. But this crisis brought out a warm, far more Latin side in everyone. A steady stream of family and friends visited us with an abundance of gifts that made the room look like a café, florist and all-night corner-shop combined. During the first two days I had scarcely eaten anything, and in lighter moments I was rather pleased by the way my waist was shrinking. It didn't last. I was urged to eat and keep up my strength. An excellent pastry shop and a delicatessen were discovered in a nearby market street. My appetite returned all too soon.

Over endless cups of tea and coffee, Antony and I would bring our visitors up to date on Nella's condition. Some had not heard how she had got ill, and sometimes I thought I simply couldn't go over the ground yet again; but I knew the opening sentences – almost the whole story – by heart; and once underway I was like the Ancient Mariner, I couldn't stop.

Nathan Ward consisted of a corridor about thirty yards long, with a pitted parquet floor. At one end was the intensive care unit, and at the other the Parents Room. In between were eight pale blue doors, leading to identical rooms large enough for a cot and a folding bed.

The intensive care unit was known as Room One to the nurses. I could still hardly believe that I was allowed to be there. Hitherto my idea of an intensive care unit (based on hazy memories of *Dr Kildare* on television) had been of a hushed room filled with gleaming technology, into which only doctors, nurses and supine patients were admitted. I thought such a place would be strictly out of bounds to visitors, whose grubby hands and shoes might pollute the sterile white surfaces.

Compared to this, Room One was very cosy. It was an irregular room, designed to accommodate four cots. The heavy swing doors were usually open, their glass panes decorated with Disney faces in poster colours (painted by children in the ward below). Inside, more baby posters and a Mothercare frieze of teddy-bears decorated the wall. Despite its cosiness, there was no lack of technology. Cupboards above and below two broad counters contained the thousands of different dressings, syringes, swabs, catheters, needles, cannulas (drip-needles) and drip tubes that are used every day – each object packed in its own sterile envelope.

Above each cot stood a bank of monitoring equipment on a deep shelf that ran round most of the room at shoulder height. The monitoring equipment shared the shelf with a few cuddly toys, boxes of tissues and a radio-cassette player. Beneath the shelf, Nella's cot was provided with a tube for oxygen and a tube for suction. Her drip bags hung from something like a black hat-stand on wheels. On the way from the drip bag to her hand, the tube carrying fluid was clipped into a black box which regulated the flow, set by the nurse on a digital display on the front panel. These drip-pumps are very sophisticated, and are designed to respond to the slightest malfunction with an urgent, insistent bleeping and a flashing light. The first time I heard it I was extremely alarmed. The nurse, however, was unimpressed. One push on the alarm turned it off, and a brief inspection of the lines revealed that the machine was only complaining about a kink in the tube.

As the hours turned into days, I got to know the nurses. Amanda was the sister on duty when Nella was admitted. She radiated calm efficiency, and was the only nurse on the ward to wear a starched collar on her royal-blue tunic. She had tight auburn curls and her pale skin was immaculately powdered. She possessed a seemingly inexhaustible well of cheerful kindness, expressed in a clear gaze and a soft voice. My spirits always lifted when she came on to the ward.

Another nurse I was particularly fond of was Craig, a young Australian with an incipient beard and a neat pony tail. His working clothes consisted of a white tunic and grey trousers, but once – when he thought he was going to be late for the 7.30 hand-over – he appeared in a pair of black cycling shorts and a T-shirt which said 'Mourn '88 – don't celebrate', a reference to the Australian bicentennial. We shared a taste for travel books and gothic novels, and I enjoyed his straight talking. I remember looking over the cassette tapes Antony and Allegra had brought, and asking

44

what he'd like to hear – by now he was as familiar with the repertoire as I was.

'Anything but those Chopin Nocturnes,' he said. 'I'm sick to death of them.'

He took great pains to make Nella comfortable. Paediatric nurses are trained to be aware of this, since their patients are often too young to express themselves; and perhaps I noticed it more in Craig because he was a male nurse. But I often saw him putting cream on her dry skin, or making rolls of gauze-lined wadding to support her neck or back.

My admiration for the nurses mounted day by day. I knew they worked long hours for little pay, but they did their work with a dedication and stamina that amazed me. I was touched by how much trouble they took to be kind to me, especially in the early days when I was often shaky and tearful. They could not offer the long-term hope I wanted. What they had, and what they tried to share with me, was a certain resilient optimism that existed independently of fluctuating hopes and fears. Talking to the nurses sometimes made me feel strangely like a schoolgirl, listening to the kindly platitudes of Brown Owl. Yet I soon found out that this frame of mind was not merely for decoration, it was vital; and that if I did not manage to acquire it, I would crack under the strain.

The nurses attributed much of their cheerfulness to the fact that they worked with children. Many of them dreaded the possibility of transferring back to adult patients. 'All those long faces, all that moaning and groaning – you have to be sympathetic, but you feel like saying come on, pull your socks up! Children don't spend so much time feeling sorry for themselves. If they are not actually feeling ill, they are playing and bouncing about – no matter what's wrong with them.'

They particularly admired Karim, an eleven-year-old Bahraini boy who was undergoing chemotherapy treatment. He endured its effect with courage, and once over, he thought no more about it. He had learnt English while in hospital, and liked wandering around the wards, visiting the friends he had made among the staff.

In the intensive care unit most of the patients were premature babies. Their frailty was encouraging to me, because it made Nella look so huge and strong. The 'premmies', as they were known, lay on their fronts in transparent perspex boxes the size of large washing-up basins. Bright lights warmed their purplish backs from above, and their tiny rib-cages heaved with the effort of each breath. They were naked except for the smallest disposable nappy which was still ten sizes too big. At first, I could not understand why each upturned bottom had '20g' or '22g' written on it. Later I found out that all nappies in the intensive care ward are weighed before and after use, to calculate fluid loss. Woolly hats were their only other garments, under which their crumpled faces were almost hidden. They looked like baby birds which had fallen out of the nest, and to me the most touching thing about these little creatures was the fluffy rabbit or duck placed in the cot, symbol of the babyhood that was waiting for them if they could survive. But to the nurses, they were already real babies. 'What's all this fuss about, you naughty boy? You think it's time for your breakfast, do you?' One of the premmies, a little girl, became very ill. When she died in the night, the sense of sadness and loss among the nurses next day was almost tangible.

Shift changes took place at 7.30 a.m., 12.30 p.m. and 9.00 p.m. Nurses who work on a paediatric intensive care unit are trained to a very high standard; yet because they were the most accessible members of this foreign world, it made a great difference to me whether they were easy to talk to or not. By having a good rapport with whoever was handling Nella, I could ask questions, even suggest things. Yet if the nurse on duty was unresponsive, I felt cut off, as though that nurse represented a barrier between me and Nella. I would remain silent, because I didn't want to antagonise her and weaken my position still further.

One person I was always particularly glad to see was Dr Trotty Kirwin, the anaesthetist, who came to see Nella every once in a while. She looked at the charts and discussed her progress with the sister, but her visits were not exclusively professional.

'I have a daughter called Eleanor too,' she said, as she looked at Nella from the end of the bed. She had an extraordinarily kind and sympathetic face. I asked her how old her daughter was. 'She's eight. I've been telling her about this little Eleanor.' The next day, Trotty arrived with a card and a knitted rabbit from her daughter. I envied Trotty: to have a healthy child represented the sum of human happiness. What would Nella be like at eight years old? I did not dare think. The fact that Trotty's child was called Eleanor made my envy all the more poignant. I imagined mother and daughter sitting at a big kitchen table, their heads close, as the little girl wrote her message to Nella.

We had now been in hospital almost a week. For Antony, Nella's illness could not have come at a worse moment, for he was finishing a book about the Battle of Crete. His deadline in seven weeks' time could not be postponed as the book was to be published on the fiftieth anniversary of the battle. Before the crisis hit us he had already been working up to fifteen hours a day, and he had to get back to work — though this did not stop him from coming into hospital at least once or twice a day.

My own life became almost monastic: stripped of all the day-to-day details that clutter it up, and dedicated to a single

47

cause which, by common consent, overrode every other obligation.

I was editing a collection of letters at the time. I called my editor Ion Trewin, told him what had happened, and said that I did not know when I would be able to get back to work. His reaction was spontaneous. 'Don't even think about the book,' he said. 'All that matters at the moment is Nella.'

However, I did keep one job in hand. I had an advance copy of a biography of the Duke of Windsor to read, because I had been asked to interview the biographer, Philip Ziegler. I was under no pressure, and before I had finished reading the book the interview was cancelled; but to me it offered an escape into another world. I needed something else to concentrate on, so that I could occasionally get away from the anxiety of Nella's illness. At first, I thought I would be quite unable to read more than a paragraph on the Duke and Duchess of Windsor; yet to my surprise, I found I could immerse myself in the lives of that dull, obsessive man and his formidable wife for whole pages at a time.

I also had my diary: a thick, page-a-day book for 1990. In January I had written about my last days of pregnancy and Nella's birth, and I started writing in it again three or four days after we came to the Westminster Children's Hospital. 'This is the book of waiting,' I wrote. 'Waiting for Nella to be born, and now waiting to see if she will live.'

Neither Antony nor I bothered to buy newspapers anymore. The news seemed too distant to hold the attention for long. But I did like looking at magazines, which people sometimes brought in and left for me. Books and magazines are silent companions. I had no desire for a radio or the television, for in my present frame of mind they would be more inclined to exasperate than entertain. I lived off sandwiches, cakes and fruit bought in the local shops. This gave me an excuse to get out, and feel part of ordinary life again – until I saw a mother with a push-chair. Then I would look with longing at the plump, healthy child inside, and wonder if its mother knew how lucky she was.

Nella began to show signs of returning consciousness in the early hours of Sunday.

'She's certainly a very resilient baby,' said Moira, the quiet Irish nurse who had been looking after her that night. 'The tranquillisers she's getting are the equivalent of a bottle of whisky to you and me, yet she's been trying to throw herself out of bed for the last three hours.'

Some part of Nella was doubtless beginning to feel uncomfortable. She had scars, stitches, two neck-lines, a peripheral line in her hand and the ileostomy. The bits of gut that had been brought to the surface of Nella's abdomen looked like two dark red, bottled cherries just above the main scar.

The larger of the two was the stoma: the upper end of the gut, which was constantly passing bright green digestive juices. These were caught in a plastic bag attached to a dressing which surrounded the stoma. The dressing was intended to prevent the liquid, which is very corrosive, seeping through on to the skin; but some liquid always seeped through, and the area around the stoma was already looking sore. (The other 'cherry' was the fistula, which marks the beginning of the lower part of the gut.)

Nella had had no food for three days after her arrival, and as a result her skin was very dry. It was peeling away in leathery sheets from her hands and, in addition, she had developed a rash from the cocktail of antibiotics, tranquillisers and blood-pressure drugs she was on. These were only the superficial problems.

The way Nella was throwing herself about was a good sign, and a scan showed that there were no obvious signs of damage to her brain; but we would not know anything for sure until she regained full consciousness.

Sunday afternoon was sunny, with a light breeze to freshen the air. Craig suggested I went for a walk in St James's Park.

'You're looking pretty peaky,' he said. 'Go on, it'll do you good. I'll look after her.'

I wandered among the tourists and families feeding bread to the ducks, and watched some sparrows flitting round the crumbs in an old man's hand. When I came back to the hospital, I felt like a prisoner returning after a day's parole.

Nella looked just as I had left her. Craig was filling in another chart. He raised his head as I came in, and smiled.

'She's woken up,' he said.

I scarcely dared believe it; but within a few minutes I saw her eyelids flicker again. Would she recognise me? The moment her eyes met mine I felt a thrill of joy, like an electric charge – there was no doubt that she knew who I was. This was the first direct contact I had had with Nella for a week. I told her how much I loved her and how wonderful it was to see her awake, while I played with her fingers and kissed them. She looked at me with great interest. Maybe she was wondering why I was crying.

'I hate to break this up,' said Craig, 'but it's time for suction.'

Since one cannot cough when attached to a ventilator, suction is essential to keep the lungs clear. Craig put on a pair of disposable gloves, tore the sterile envelope off a fresh suction tube and fitted it to the tap above Nella's bed. I had seen it done many times before in the past few days – but then she had been unconscious. A look of horror crossed her face as he put the tube down the pipe already in her nose, and as it was fed into her lungs her back arched, and she struggled and gagged. There was a horrible sucking noise, and then Craig gently pulled it out. My heart nearly broke as Nella's face crumpled and she tried to cry – but no sound came: the ventilator stops the vocal chords. All one could hear was her breath.

She calmed down when I gave her a dummy, and relapsed into an uneasy sleep. A little later, she started fiddling about with the dummy – not as easy as it used to be, for one hand was bandaged on to a pale blue plastic splint which held the cannula in place. I watched with mounting delight as she put it in the wrong way round, took it out to see what was wrong, twiddled it about again and finally put it in the right way: a small feat but, to me, conclusive proof that she had suffered no brain damage.

I had longed so much for Nella to regain consciousness; but now that she had, I often wished she could drift back into that warm dark oblivion where nothing could hurt her. It would certainly have made life easier for both of us. Fully conscious, she had to suffer the ordeal of daily blood samples, the stinging sensation of antibiotics being pumped into tiny veins, the itchy pain of the stitches in her neck and abdomen, and the cumbersome ileostomy dressing. Perhaps she did not feel all of these things, but I felt them for her. As well as the rash, she had a large pressure sore on the back of her head, for she could not move her head much while on the ventilator. And on top of all this, the doctors were beginning to decrease the pain-killers, tranquillisers and blood-pressure regulating drugs she had been on. She must have felt she had woken up in hell.

What made her most uncomfortable, I think, was the ventilator. The bandages round her head and the attachment that kept the tube clipped in her nose exerted a constant pressure. Worst of all was the invasive tube into her throat which took away the only power she had – the power to make a noise. The other thing I hated about the ventila-

tor was that it partly hid her face, and the bandages changed
the shape of her head. She would not look like the Nella I
knew until it was taken off.

Suction was done every two hours, and now she could see
it coming. She would start to breathe faster and shake her
head from side to side the moment she saw the nurse put on
disposable gloves. While it was actually happening I would
lean right over the bed, hold her hands and put my face
close to her head, so that I could be as near as possible
without having to watch.

On Monday, Clare came back. Antony met her train at
Victoria and, as he drove the short distance to the hospital,
he tried to warn her of what to expect by describing all the
invasive technology Nella was attached to.

Clare looked remarkably composed when she saw Nella
in Nathan Ward for the first time, though in fact she was
profoundly shaken. Nothing could have prepared her for
Nella's sad, frightened eyes behind the ventilator. It was
only her determination not to upset Nella or myself that
stopped her from bursting into tears.

From then on, Clare came in every weekday to sit with
Nella. The bond between them became even stronger, and
Clare's presence took an immense amount of pressure off
me at a time when I had never felt so tired and emotionally
drained.

Throughout Monday Nella became more and more tense
and nervous. By the evening she was so frightened and
upset by all the different things that had to be done to her,
that I longed to put my hand on the arm of the nurse or
doctor and say 'Please, don't do it, just this once. Give her a
break.' My empathy with Nella's pain and distress became
more and more acute, like a rising hysteria. I was exhausted,
but I could hardly bear to leave her with the night-nurse.
My mother finally persuaded me to go to bed by promising
that she would stay with Nella until she fell asleep. She did
not get home until past one o'clock.

Early the following morning, while I had gone out to buy breakfast and before Clare arrived, the ventilator was removed. A nurse in the corridor told me the good news when I got back, and I hurried into Room One to see Nella. Sticky white adhesive still clung to her forehead, and there was a sore patch where the tube had been; yet to me she looked wonderful, and I kissed her forehead and the bridge of her nose again and again. Nella looked utterly bewildered; but at least she could hear herself making a noise, even if it was only a very faint croak. She was hoarse for the next four or five weeks.

Nella spent much of Wednesday asleep. Recovery sleep, they call it – deep, healing sleep. I spent a lot of time just looking at her. They put another tube down her nose and into her stomach, but it was much finer and softer than the ventilator tube. Her hair was beginning to fall out now, as a result of one of the drugs. She was left with a thin fuzz, except for the area on the pressure sore, where the hair was gripped in place by the large red scab that was forming.

So many people came up to reassure me her hair would grow back that I began to feel they were hiding something; but further questioning revealed that a baby's hair loss often provokes unreasonable anxiety in the mother, who transfers many of her worries about the child to its bald head.

On Wednesday we went out to dinner with friends. We had been out once or twice for family suppers over the past few days, but this was the first dinner party since Nella had become ill. Antony felt it would do us both good and was looking forward to it but I wasn't, and on the way there the prospect of a room full of people filled me with increasing dread. I felt emotionally flayed – I had a skin too few, I couldn't face it. I started crying.

Once out of the car we walked around for a bit, and the fresh air revived me. I still felt wobbly when we went in but a couple of glasses of wine helped, and by the time we sat down I was really quite enjoying myself. I did not want to talk about Nella – not because I was afraid of bursting into tears, but for fear of becoming a hospital bore. I held out until the second course, when my neighbour said he had heard our daughter was ill and asked how she was. I was determined to be brief, but despite his rapidly glazing eyes I could not stop until my tale was told.

Nella was still very miserable, but she had good moments too. The day after the dinner party, she smiled. A proper smile, looking me full in the face. I held her hand, and to my surprise I found myself talking about what fun it would be when she was home again, and what we would do. I had been repressing all such cosy thoughts: they risked tempting fate. After all, Nella was still extremely ill. She would have to be fed intravenously for a very long time, and her gut was so badly damaged that no one was prepared to predict whether or not it would ever heal. Yet Nella's smile, brief as it was, had given me a surge of encouragement I could not suppress. She looked at me very intently, not wanting to miss a word as I babbled on.

Since the ventilator had been removed, I was also allowed to cuddle Nella on my lap from time to time. It was quite a business. I sat down in the armchair, and then the nurse had to arrange the lines connecting her to the monitors.

'Now we'll put this one here, and that one comes round here, and . . . hello, here's a new one since I was here last. Where does this go? Whoops, there goes an electrode.' At this point the monitor beeped urgently. 'Oh shut up, you!'

She pressed a button and the noise stopped. 'All three electrodes have got to be changed anyway, so let's take them off and I'll put them on again when she's back in bed. Now where was I . . . yes, so this one comes here . . . are you settled comfortably? Right, here we come.'

Nella was lifted gently from the bed and put into my arms in one smooth motion.

At first I was so nervous of pulling something out, I hardly dared breathe; but soon I was picking at the sticky grey residue that clung around her forehead, from the adhesive bandage that had kept the miner's lamp in place. It was such a joy to feel the weight of her in my arms again, see her whole face, and hear her soft, hoarse voice chattering and grumbling at me. I would watch her, enchanted – and then come to with a jolt as she nearly yanked the tube out of her nose, or tugged at the bandaged splint on her hand.

CHAPTER SIX

O N Friday morning, Antony and I – and my father, who was visiting at the time – were invited to the office of Dr Peter Sullivan, the Lecturer in Child Health. Dr Sullivan was the senior doctor on Nella's case after the consultant, Dr Brueton. I put him in his late thirties; but his slim build and expression of intense alertness will keep him looking that age for a long time, so he may have been older.

We walked across the road from the main hospital to his office which was in a tall, narrow house with steep stairs. It contained a computer and a large desk, on which stood a microscope. Among the textbooks above his head was a boxed software package with 'GASTRO-SOFT' written in large letters on the spine. I wondered about Gastro-soft while Dr Sullivan went off to find another chair. When we were all seated, he began.

'First of all I'd like to tell you something about the histology of the gut.' He had a faint Lancashire accent and a nice sense of irony. 'May I assume your total ignorance of the subject?' Our assent was emphatic.

One learns wonderful things in hospital. In section, the gut looks like a rolled-up carpet, pile side inward. The 'pile' is made up of thousands of thin projections called villi. The outermost cells on each projection are what absorb the food travelling through the gut and, in an adult, their combined surface area would cover a tennis court. New cells are constantly being made in cell-factories called crypts, which lie in the wall of the gut itself. As new cells work their way up into the villi, the old cells on the surface drop off. As a result of this continuous process, the 'tennis court' is replaced every thirty-six hours.

After a bad attack of gastro-enteritis, the projecting villi are left looking more like stumps – yet the gradual reintroduction of food stimulates the crypts into making new cells. The villi start growing again, and the lining of the gut returns to normal. The trouble was that Nella's gut had been so badly damaged it could not tolerate food of any kind.

Something else had to be found to stimulate the crypts to start making cells again, and the answer, he told us, might lie in Epidermal Growth Factor (EGF). This is a synthetic hormone, the product of recombinant DNA technology. It is a substance which mirrors, molecule for molecule, the hormone used by the body to regenerate damaged tissue. EGF was still in the experimental stage; but Dr Sullivan had located a batch of it at the Cambridge laboratory where he used to work. Because it was not yet being made in commercial quantities, its price was calculated in terms of research time – in other words, in tens of thousands of pounds. Dr Sullivan had contacted ICI, to whom it belonged, and outlined Nella's unusual case and the reasons for trying EGF. Very generously, ICI donated the EGF necessary for the treatment.

He went on to explain that EGF had been tested, with mixed results, on babies with congenital gut disorders. Nella, on the other hand, had been born with a perfectly good gut: so perhaps the EGF treatment would stand a better chance. Nella's case would be followed by Professor Nicholas Wright, the Director of Histopathology at the Hammersmith Hospital. He had done a great deal of research into EGF, and was the acknowledged expert on its effect in the gut.

Dr Sullivan emphasised that this treatment had never

been attempted in a case like hers. The decision to try EGF had been taken after much consultation since it was not in the textbooks. The textbooks say that guts as badly damaged as Nella's must be cut out.

I asked if it had ever been used on other sorts of cases.

'The Americans have been using it to treat burns,' said Dr Sullivan. 'Stimulated by EGF, the skin seems to heal remarkably quickly. We might find that it helps Nella's skin too – it will be interesting to see.'

Antony and I were all for trying this EGF, but we had one question: 'What are the likely side-effects?'

'Probably none, at this dosage. This is a natural product, like plasma or insulin. In theory, the worst that can happen is that it won't work.'

I walked with Antony to where he had left his bicycle. Now that the immediate crisis was over, he had returned to work. Yet despite the intense pressure he was under, he often made the time to relieve Clare for her lunch-break, and filled in at weekends with Kinta and Anne, myself, and other friends. He telephoned every morning at eight, to find out how Nella had passed the night, and remained on instant standby. When I needed him, a tearful telephone call brought him round to the hospital in fifteen minutes.

Antony had always seen Nella's situation more clearly than I did. I had left Dr Sullivan's office buoyed up with new hope, an emotion that Antony now treated with the utmost suspicion: hopes had turned to ashes so often during the last few days.

'Remember,' he said, 'it might not work.'

'But even if it doesn't, we won't have lost anything,' I replied.

'Yes, but think what that will mean. She'll have to undergo another bout of major surgery, and they'll have to cut out a good part of her gut.'

Yet he had spared me his worst fears – fears that were well-founded. If the EGF did not work, not only would Nella have to go back into surgery, she would also be left with a gut that could not absorb food. She might have to spend her life in hospital, being fed intravenously.

Another bout of surgery, to cut out much of her gut! My invisible blinkers had been so effective that although I knew this was a possibility, the reality of it had not hit me until now. I felt as though a large stone had been dropped into my stomach.

I walked back up the stairs to Nathan Ward. The stairwell was the hospital's art gallery, plastered with pictures and projects done by children attending the Westminster Children's Hospital School. The paintings were bright and confident, encrusted with glitter, cotton-wool, chocolate-foil and collages of coloured paper. The projects were more serious, laid out neatly on white paper with scientific drawings in pencil. 'Magnetism: here's what happened when Amina, Bob, Nabil and Mandy lowered a magnet into a) a bowl of pins b) a plate of iron filings.'

On the second landing was a payphone, into which mothers spilled out the hopes, fears and frustrations that punctuate the long days of waiting. The tales the payphone heard might have been more cheerful if one could have gazed at the paintings while talking. As it was, the miserly eighteen inches of cable kept the caller tethered to the receiver and looking into a grimy light-well of bare brick walls supporting a network of pipes. A corrugated-iron-clad chimney rose beyond. The base of the light-well was formed by a conical roof made of sections of grimy plate glass, while the top was netted to prohibit nesting pigeons. The pigeons still managed to use it as a latrine, and everywhere were speckles of soot-blackened guano. If any view in the hospital could be calculated to depress the spirits, this was it.

The rest of the day was a nightmare, with Nella having to undergo one thing after another. First the line in her hand collapsed, so another had to be found – either in her other hand or an ankle. They tried again and again without success, and finally had to site it in the scalp. The only way to keep a needle in there was to make a little hat out of a soft plastic bowl and tie it under her chin; but this made her so miserably uncomfortable that she wriggled around until the needle was dislodged, and the whole process had to be gone through again. Finally they found a vein in her foot. When all that was over, we noticed that gastric juices from the stoma had been leaking under the dressing. Her skin was burnt so raw that it wept blood and water. The dressing was removed, and then Dr Sullivan said he would do a biopsy, which meant taking a sample sliver off the stoma.

The sample had to be treated with chemicals as soon as possible. Dr Sullivan thought he had everything he needed in a laboratory upstairs, but at the last moment they discovered that someone had moved it all. A trainee doctor was dispatched to get the necessary chemicals and equipment from the main hospital, and poor Nella had to wait there without a dressing as corrosive liquid oozed out of her stoma. The only thing we could do to relieve her was to put vaseline on the skin, and pray that the doctor would come back soon. In the end her errand took two hours, during which there was the usual routine of nappy changes and suction, which still had to be done despite the fact that Nella was off the ventilator. Once the doctor returned, there was a further delay before Dr Sullivan was free to do the biopsy, and when that was finished they had to take blood again. The task was given to a gentle, nervous young woman who had only recently qualified, and the sight of her trying to squeeze blood out of that poor bruised arm was almost too much for me. I held on to Nella, and tried to put as much reassurance and encouragement into my voice as I could. I felt I was collaborating in the torture, and worst of all, that Nella's trust and confidence in me might be shattered. I looked up, and met the steady gaze of Dr Sullivan.

'Hard, isn't it?' he said simply. The understanding in his voice brought me more comfort than a whole speech of kind words.

I think Nella fell into an exhausted sleep in the mid-afternoon, but I was so wound up I could do nothing. I felt cold and sweaty. Thoughts jangled in my head, and the muscles in my neck and shoulder were as taut as high-tension cables. I was also worried about Nella's temperature, which had been very high since three o'clock. I telephoned Antony, and poured out the horrors of the last few hours. Antony not only sympathised; he always made me feel loved and understood, and his emotional support gave me the courage to carry on. He told me he would be at the hospital by seven. Then I called the healer and told her about Nella's high temperature. 'We'll get on to it right away,' she said. I felt better: whatever happened, all fronts had been covered.

When Antony arrived we went out for supper, leaving Nella with Allegra. Antony rather fancied some fish and chips but I couldn't face fried food, so we ended up with a vegetable bake dominated by the taste of half-cooked onion, in a stripped-pine basement smelling faintly of incense and boiled beans. We walked back to the hospital wishing we'd had the fish and chips, wishing we were at home with Nella tucked up in her own cot. I went to bed at nine, took two sleeping pills and slept blissful black emptiness till morning.

A car was sent to Cambridge to collect the frozen EGF. I never saw it, but I thought about it a lot. I imagined a hard, pale gold liquid in a tiny frost-covered vial, surrounded by freezer packs and encased in polystyrene. I wondered about the driver. How much had he been told? I would like to

think that a skilled technician had put the package rever-
ently into his hands saying, 'Here is a very precious drug
worth thousands of pounds. We hope it will save a baby's
life, so drive very carefully.' But the package was more likely
to have been handed to him by a security guard, who might
have remarked 'Here you are, keep it this way up.'

Nella's EGF treatment started on the weekend of the
fifteenth and sixteenth of September, and the superficial
effects were startling. Within twenty-four hours, her skin
looked far less dry than before; and the raw and inflamed
area around the stoma began to heal. I was even more
amazed when I heard that the quantity of EGF needed for
Nella's six-day treatment was so tiny, it was measured in
nanograms – in other words, in millionths of a gram.

The EGF was held in solution in a large, six-inch cylinder,
with its own built-in line. The cylinder was attached to a
timer-pump, and dripped into Nella at the rate of one
milli-litre an hour. When it was finished the timer started
bleeping, and the empty cylinder was replaced by a full one.

I watched Dana, one of the many Australian nurses who
worked at the hospital through an agency, perform the
change-over with the sister in charge, following the normal
hospital procedure.

Both nurses put on sterile gloves. The sister held her
hands in the air like a surgeon while Dana removed tweez-
ers, cotton-wool and miniature sterilising bowls from their
sterile pouches. Only then was the sister ready to unscrew
the old EGF line from the connecting tap attached to Nella's
hand, and screw in the new one. The operation took the best
part of ten minutes, and was quite painless for Nella. EGF
does not sting like antibiotics.

When the task was done, Dana took off her gloves. I liked
Dana a lot. She was friendly and very fond of Nella. She had
a broad face with beautiful green eyes, red hair and a fringe.

'So this is the magic stuff, eh?' She picked up the empty

EGF cylinder, and shook it on to her hand like a bottle of hand-lotion. Out came a drop or two. 'Let's see what it can do for my hang-nails.'

CHAPTER SEVEN

BOTH Antony and I felt a tremendous admiration for the way Nella had endured the past two weeks. It seemed monstrously unfair that a baby should be stricken by an illness so savage that only the harshest treatment could hold it at bay. She was only eight months old; yet she had suffered more pain, and fought harder for life, than either of her parents. What she had been through made her doubly precious, and her courage gave us strength.

On Monday, 17 September, Nella – in her cot, accompanied by her drips on their black metal hat-stand – was wheeled out of intensive care, and along the corridor to Room Eight. As I walked beside her, every step away from Room One felt like a step forward.

But the move also meant that I had to relinquish the luxury of the Parents Room. I was offered a room in the Parents Unit on the floor above, which I would share with another mother; or I could sleep beside Nella on a folding bed in her room. I chose the latter. I wanted to be with her at night, since now she no longer had a nurse to herself; whoever was in charge might not be free to come at once if she woke up in fear or pain.

Behind its pale blue door, Room Eight measured about seven feet by twelve. It contained a wash-basin, a locker, an armchair and a small trolley; and once Nella's cot was in place with her drips beside her, plus my collapsible bed, the remaining space was as narrow as the corridor of a railway carriage.

It looked even fuller by the time I had brought some things from home: my own duvet and pillows, tea, biscuits, and a lamp which I set on the locker, so that we did not always have to be under the glare of the fluorescent lights in the ceiling. I also brought some more toys for Nella, and taped her Get Well cards to the high bars of her cot.

I had two books with me. Vita Sackville-West's *The Eagle and the Dove*, the lives of two contemplatives; and Bruce Chatwin's *The Songlines*, the contemplations of a traveller on the nomadic roots of the human race. Both books were relatively short. The constant interruptions of hospital life mean that one cannot read for long, and babies – ill or not – are demanding companions. This was definitely not the moment to embark on Proust.

The window in Nella's room was large; but it was separated from the open air by a long gallery, some four or five feet wide, added to the exterior of the building. This housed the ward's toys – an astonishing profusion of plastic musical boxes, mobiles, balls, bricks, rattles and activity boards. The gallery was mostly glass, through which one could see the plane trees in Vincent Square. I listened to the leaves rustling at night, and thought wistfully about woods and bracken and damp fresh air.

Trotty had warned me that Nella would be very bolshy for a while after leaving intensive care, for that was when the pain-killers and tranquillisers – which had been gradually reduced over the past few days – were stopped altogether. No longer cushioned by drugs and still adjusting to consciousness, Nella was bound to feel withdrawal symptoms. 'Be prepared,' said Trotty. 'Sometimes the reaction is so dramatic, it seems like a complete personality change – you may not recognise her.' She assured me that the effects wore off in time. I was grateful for her warning, though it provoked anxious thoughts. I feared that Nella's ordeal might have filled her with anger and resentment, or left her with a permanent horror of being touched.

Nella was terribly restless and cried for much of that first night. She was given paracetamol every four hours, but she never slept for longer than an hour and a half.

The room was very hot. A radiator which could not be turned off ran the entire length of one wall, and there was no choice but to lie next to it. Nella's cot was nearest the window so I don't think the heat bothered her much, but I felt suffocated.

The night-nurse came in every two hours to do 'obs' (observations), which meant checking the pumps and taking Nella's temperature. Every four hours, Nella had antibiotics. One lot was injected directly into a cannula, usually sited in a hand or foot. It stung, and Nella cried. I can still hear that cry: a wheezing, repetitive sob, her lungs working like bellows, her body tense, back arched.

More antibiotics had to be infused over half an hour, which meant rigging them up to a time-pump. These antibiotics did not sting; but when the pump was empty, it started to beep, just after Nella had drifted off to sleep, and it beeped and beeped till the nurse came to silence it and detach the pump. It took several days before I acquired the confidence to turn the beepers off myself.

Once the antibiotics had been administered, I thought we would be left in peace – but the next time the nurse came in to do obs, she brought the blood-pressure machine with her. I hated this machine. It consisted of a blue box on a stand, with a digital display and an arm-band on the end of a rubber tube – specially designed for infants. On Nella, this contraption did not work well. The arm-band inflated automatically, and exerted such pressure on her arm that it made her cry – at which point the machine seized up and refused to give a reading. So the whole thing had to be done again, and again, before the nurse finally gave up. 'Never mind,' she'd say cheerfully, 'I'll pop back in half an hour and we'll have another go, shall we?' At two in the morning with a hysterical baby to soothe, it was not a pleasant prospect.

The blood-pressure machine was state-of-the-art technology, I was told, and very expensive. It bore a little brass plaque, stating that it had been bought with funds raised by a charity ball. As I tried to coax Nella to sleep, the thought of those well-dressed, well-meaning people who had danced all night to pay for it made me furious.

I had not expected to sleep, but I couldn't even doze for long. My few moments of lying down were wrecked by the knowledge that someone would come in sooner or later, or Nella – who tossed and turned incessantly – would start crying again. Across the corridor was the sister's room, and the nurses chatted happily in the corridor. The baby in the room opposite ours cried for what seemed like hours at a time. I shut the door to try and deaden the noise a bit; but any nurse who came in invariably left it ajar.

As the night wore on, the ward became quiet, sometimes almost silent. Nella's restlessness gave way to a peaceful exhaustion, and she fell asleep around dawn. I managed to persuade the nurse to postpone the next obs till she woke up, hoping this would give us an hour or two of uninterrupted sleep – but at seven sharp, the cleaning lady came in to empty the rubbish bins. We woke to the clank of metal, and the crackle of stiff yellow plastic bin-liners.

I dozed off again, till the click of a switch and a sudden electric hum announced that someone had turned on the fluorescent lights overhead. It was Dr Khan. Her slightly apologetic air implied that she was recently qualified. She held a miniature cardboard tray on which were two phials, a syringe and a needle. 'I have to take some blood,' she said with a shy smile.

Specimens of blood and urine were taken every day, mainly for the technicians who made up Nella's intravenous food: the ingredients were adjusted according to the information gained from the samples. In Room One, I was usually told when blood-taking was imminent so I could make myself scarce, but this morning I was taken by surprise.

I scrambled out of bed, put on my dressing-gown and went to find a nurse to hold Nella while it was being done. Once out of the room, I did not return until it was all over. I felt a traitor leaving her alone, but two thoughts eased my troubled conscience a little. A psychiatrist friend told me that, for the sake of our future relationship, it was just as well that Nella did not see me as a willing collaborator in her daily ordeal. My absence also made it much easier on the doctor. The ones who appeared early in the morning were young, and still gaining experience: taking blood from a baby is not a pleasant job, and the last thing they need is the presence of the baby's mother, gasping and wincing with every jab of the needle.

I made myself a cup of tea in the little kitchen, and took it hesitantly into the intensive care room. I did not know whether I was still allowed in, now that Nella was no longer there, but no one objected. Wendy, the sister in charge, was feeding one of the premmies, a job which involved holding aloft a tiny syringe of formula while it trickled down a naso-gastric tube to the baby's stomach. The baby wriggled feebly, making swallowing and sucking noises. Its eyes were tight shut.

Wendy had a sympathetic and motherly manner, enhanced by her royal-blue uniform, which came well below her knees. It was quite a revelation when I saw her going off duty one day: her fair hair, normally tied back in a clip, cascaded about her shoulders. She wore a short skirt and a big black leather jacket, and her sensible black lace-ups had turned into high heels.

'Hello there! How's Nella?' she asked.

'As well as can be expected, I suppose. She's very irritable. I think the ileostomy dressing is leaking.'

'And how about you?'

I told her all about my dreadful night. Lying next to the radiator had given me a splitting headache, and I was light-headed from lack of sleep.

'Still, you seem to be coping all right,' she said.

'I can't cope with watching Nella's blood being taken, and I don't know how long I'll be able to cope with nights like last night.'

'What I meant was, you don't seem anxious about having left intensive care. Some mums get really upset – they feel they've been abandoned.' I must have looked puzzled. 'They feel overwhelmed by the responsibility of being in a room alone with their sick baby, without a nurse.'

I looked down the corridor, and saw Dr Khan returning with her little cardboard tray. 'All over,' she smiled, as relieved as I was.

I hurried back to the room. Nella glanced up briefly as I came in, and then resumed her examination of whatever was in her hands. I kissed the top of her head. The occasional quick intake of breath and her wet eyes showed she had been crying, but it was all over now, and she seemed calm. For a moment, I could not identify the crackly thing she was playing with. It proved to be the plastic wrapper off a syringe.

At ten o'clock, Clare took over, having taken the Underground from Fulham – a routine we were to follow throughout the coming weeks. Clare had been quick to get over her initial shock at seeing Nella in hospital and, unlike me, she was strong enough to stay with Nella when the doctor had to find a new vein in her hand or foot. Nella could now sit up in her baby chair, which made a great difference to her life. Clare found things in the toy gallery for Nella to play with, and often told her stories and read to her. While Nella was asleep, she read magazines and chatted to the nurses. The time passed quickly enough if Nella was feeling well; but the days when she was grizzly and unsettled were long and hard. Yet Clare took each day as it came, without complaint. I was not the only person who appreciated Clare's cheerfulness and constancy: as soon as she came in, Nella would greet her with smiles and coos of pleasure.

Before going home to catch up on sleep during the day, I often lingered on in the hope of seeing Dr Brueton or Dr Sullivan. My relationship with the doctors had gone on to a different footing, now that I no longer needed the degree of time and patience they had given me when Nella was in acute danger. They still took time to answer my questions and explain how Nella's treatment was progressing; but they were brisker, more business-like. Dr Brueton only appeared on his scheduled rounds, at the head of a dozen people including the psychologist, the pharmacist and the dietician. The everyday questions concerning Nella's treatment I would put to Dr Sullivan, who was now in immediate charge of the case.

He was a born teacher: clear and patient with parents like me who had been thrown into an alien world, brisk with the graduates. I remember him asking one of the newly qualified doctors on his team to describe Nella's condition. The young man took a deep breath and began, but was interrupted before the end of his first sentence.

'No, no, no, Doctor! Everything *must* come in the right order. First I want to hear about the respiratory system, then the cardio-vascular, and *then* you can discuss other organs.'

Only once had I seen Dr Sullivan look disorganised. We had been talking by Nella's bedside one Sunday morning, while she was still in intensive care, when he was called to the telephone.

'Oh no!' he groaned, and sat down in a chair by the desk.

'I am so sorry. Look, I'll be finished here in half an hour, I'll come straight round ... Are you sure? ... OK then ... See you later.'

He put down the telephone and came back to resume our conversation with a rather shame-faced smile. 'That was my wife,' he explained. 'I've managed to lock her out of the house.'

On the day after Nella was moved into the little room, Dr Sullivan said he would take another biopsy from her stoma that afternoon. He suggested that Antony and I might like to look at the slide with him through a microscope, before he sent it off to the lab. I told him that Antony would be there; but that I was due to have a long massage at home, which I sorely needed.

Having a full body massage while your child is seriously ill in hospital may sound like gross self-indulgence, but it was the best thing I could have done. The last ten days had twisted my nerves and muscles into a knot which I could not unravel without help, and had left me tense and irritable. For everybody's sake, I needed to relax.

The massage was done by Sarah Young, a therapist who visits her clients at home, for she believes that the benefit of a massage is greatly increased if you can rest properly afterwards. She took her time, working from my feet upwards. At first, my muscles were so tight that they felt like stone; but gradually the tension melted, and I began to enjoy the warmth and well-being that her hands seemed to be rubbing back into my legs and arms. She said she could feel an area of cold in the middle of my body, a sure sign that my reserves of physical and emotional energy were extremely low.

After about an hour and a half, I felt very relaxed. My eyes were closed; and while Sarah was massaging my head and face, I had a vivid image of Nella. I could see her with extraordinary clarity, though we were separated by what seemed like infinite space, and a vast abyss filled with wispy stuff like cloud. Nella did not seem to mind. She smiled and waved encouragingly, and the sight of her looking so happy and loving filled me with joy. At the same time, she seemed so totally separate from me that I could not reach her. I found myself crying, the tears pouring down my face – a positive torrent of pent-up emotion, which Sarah's hands had somehow unleashed.

Sarah left me tucked up in bed, with several jerseys on. I drifted into a warm dark day-dream in which I imagined the void within me, where all my reserves of energy used to be. It was enormous, like the inside of the Colosseum, and broken as if by bombs; but its steep walls were being repaired, by unseen hands, with hundreds of tiny bricks of a deep, translucent blue.

As I lay resting in bed, Antony set off on his bicycle to join Dr Sullivan and see the biopsy. Despite his belief in the need for pre-emptive pessimism, he could not help feeling excited and instinctively confident of the outcome. He rushed up to join Nella and Clare but, in true hospital fashion, a long wait soon brought him down to a more sober frame of mind and reawakened uncertainties, especially the thought of her extremely limited life should the EGF fail. Both he and Clare became nervous in their impatience, but had to hide this in order not to upset Nella. More urgent matters were keeping Dr Sullivan, and nearly two hours passed before the other emergency had been dealt with.

When Dr Sullivan arrived, he rubbed his hands as he considered the sequence of events for taking a sample from Nella's ileostomy. He hoped that a quick look at it through a microscope might give him some idea of the way things were going; but before any detailed analysis could be undertaken, the sample had to be dissected, stained, and mounted by a skilled lab technician.

The microscope was set up on a table in the intensive care room – there was certainly not enough space in Nella's cubicle. Antony and Clare held Nella's arms out of the way while Dr Sullivan snipped the sliver of tissue from the ileostomy with an instrument that looked like a minute cigar-cutter. He assured Antony and Clare that there were no nerves in the gut and she would feel nothing, but Nella was naturally upset by this further assault on her poor battered body. They comforted her while Dr Sullivan put the sliver of tissue into a miniature bottle. Then he hurried up the corridor to the intensive care room with Antony close behind.

Once there, Dr Sullivan transferred the sliver on to a glass slide with what seemed like interminable precision, and then there was a lot of aligning and adjusting to be done. The nurses gave Antony encouraging smiles as he stood around, trying to keep out of the way, yet ready to dash forward and glance through the microscope. Finally, Dr Sullivan took off his spectacles and peered down the black tube. Antony was bursting to ask his opinion. Dr Sullivan took a slow, deep breath, and exhaled in a way that indicated satisfaction.

'Are there grounds for cautious optimism?' said Antony, resorting to formula with a smile.

'Yes,' said Dr Sullivan, jumping up, and gesturing for him to take a look himself. 'Very cautious optimism.' But Dr Sullivan's uncontainable grin more than belied his choice of words. Antony, blinking and squinting, found it extremely hard to distinguish what he was supposed to be looking for in the red and pink kaleidoscope at the other end of the microscope.

Dr Sullivan explained that there were, as yet, no signs of villi – those filaments which absorb food. One could not expect to see them at this stage. However, the tissue of the gut wall did look incomparably healthier than that of the pre-treatment sample. Antony nodded earnestly at everything he was told, but was guided more by Dr Sullivan's inability to keep a suitably detached expression on his face than by scientific explanation. In fact Dr Sullivan's enthusiasm was so manifest that the formula of 'cautious optimism' became something of a running joke between them.

The slide was labelled and taken off to the laboratory, and Dr Sullivan had to hurry off to another ward. Antony agonised between the desire to ring me, and the fear of waking me. He woke me up.

There is nothing like waking up to good news for making one feel like springing out of bed. I felt absurdly happy, and – after the massage – better than I had felt for a long time.

I found Kinta, who was getting ready to go to the hospital for the early evening shift. All the to-ing and fro-ing between Fulham and the hospital was taking its toll on her, and although she never complained, we worried that she was overdoing things; yet the renewed hope of Antony's message seemed to revitalise her completely.

My next thought was to pick up the telephone and tell everyone I could think of; but I forced myself to remember that it was not really good news yet, only an encouraging start. I could not afford to tempt fate.

Nella seemed rather bemused by the delighted hugs and kisses she received that evening. Her life had not changed much since the biopsy, but I noticed that she was in a very good mood. I wondered if this was in response to our own raised spirits.

CHAPTER EIGHT

NELLA adapted well to her new life in Room Eight. She spent some of her time sitting up in her baby chair, wearing no more than a nappy and a cotton blanket, which covered her from the waist down. The blanket kept her attention away from the ileostomy bag, its dressing and her scar, and made her look more presentable. She had one cannula, sited in a hand or a foot, which was kept in place by a bandage round a pale blue splint. Nella did sometimes pick at this, but very rarely. She tended to pick at the bag only when the dressing was old, and the corrosive fluid had begun to leak on to her skin.

The lines in her neck had been removed while she was still in intensive care, and she now had a long line just below her shoulder: four inches of needle-thin, flexible steel tube which had been pushed into the muscle tissue. This was done under general anaesthetic, a few days after her third operation. On the surface of her body, the thin metal tube was linked up to the plastic tube carrying the food by a savage-looking piece of hard plastic which reminded me of a rawl-plug. It was very visible, being covered only by a transparent adhesive dressing, and there were red patches where it dug into the soft flesh. It really did dig, too: the red patches turned to three tiny scars which she still bears. The intravenous food (known as TPN, short for total parenteral nutrition) was carried in two thin plastic tubes, one white and one clear, which joined up before they went into the long line. We tried to keep these tubes out of the way, but they often fell on to her arm or over her chest.

To me it was extraordinary how little attention she paid to any of this invasive technology. Putting myself in the same position, I imagined the itchy pain of irritated flesh, the cumbersome bag, the hard ileostomy dressing with the raw skin beneath. I saw my temper getting worse and worse as I fought the ever-increasing temptation to scratch and pick, how I would snap at the nurses and moan to my visitors – yet Nella did not seem particularly bothered by it all. I marvelled at the elasticity of her mind, its power of absorption. Once she had accepted the needles and tubes as extensions of her body, she simply forgot about them. On the few occasions when she did start pulling the lines or fiddling with her cannula, she was easily distracted.

I was also amazed by how happily she passed the time. She could not read or watch television, and there were no meals to punctuate her day. Yet she cooed and grunted and babbled away in the unquestioned, immediate present of childhood, and played with her toys. She had only two positions, sitting up or lying down, and her only form of energetic exercise was to kick her legs. Yet as the illness had struck before she had learnt to crawl, the restriction of movement did not bother her much either.

Her favourite objects were the crackly sterile packages for syringes and dressings, and a transparent ball inside which a duck floated in water. She shook the ball, and then watched intently as the duck bobbed up and down. Then she would turn to her stuffed Noah's Ark, which carried six printed cotton animals each in its own pocket. Nella enjoyed taking the animals out but made no attempt to put them back in, and one or more of them were always on the floor. I was forever crawling behind the cot to pick them up, which Nella found very entertaining. A furry Peter Rabbit was particularly popular when somebody wound him up and played the tune, but her other soft toys were of no interest unless they were made to do things, like dance or fall off the top of the cot. Her first two teeth were just emerging, and when Nella had nothing better to do she would pull down one of her Get Well cards and chew it. I remember being dreadfully anxious one day, when strange dark flecks appeared in the ileostomy bag. They turned out to be fragments of Get Well card.

She was easily tired. When the coos and babbles gave way to a plaintive whinge, I would lie her down, close the curtains, and play soothing music on the tape recorder until she dozed off. Sometimes I would lie her on her side, and massage her back with baby oil. If she was tired and miserable, I would bring the armchair close to the bed. Then, being very careful of the lines, I would lift Nella out of her cot, sit down, and rock her in my arms. I sang her songs I had learnt from my father, and a song of my own invention called the Nathan Ward song. Medically speaking it is not very accurate, but I only ever sang it to Nella.

> Oh the doctors and the nurses
> They all say Nella's doing well
> And now thanks to the stuff from Cambridge
> We've knocked those bugs to hell.
> The day that we go home, my love
> Will be of all days the best
> But till then we're stuck here in Nathan Ward
> Just trying to get some rest.

It went to the tune of *Annie Laurie*, one of a choice of eight tunes on a baby-blue plastic Japanese musical box. Clare had found it in the ward's gallery of toys, and fixed it to the end of Nella's bed. The musical box was battery-operated, and would carry on playing the chosen tune until stopped manually. Mercifully, it also had volume control. I would sing the Nathan Ward song over and over again, rocking Nella in my arms, while *Annie Laurie* played very softly in the background. Then, when she was nearly asleep, I would put her back in the cot.

On one of his Tuesday rounds, Dr Brueton brought up the subject of regression. From the way he chose his words, I understood that he felt the subject required tact.

'You see, Nella has undergone three operations, she has been in a coma, and she has been subjected to a powerful barrage of drugs. It would not be surprising if she had regressed a little in her development – in fact we would expect it. There is a good chance that she'll catch up; but perhaps you've noticed that she is not ... quite as adept as she was before.'

I thought about this carefully, but said I could not see much difference.

'She can still pull Antony's glasses off, turn the pages of her books, and put anything and everything into her mouth ... No, I can't see any regression.'

Dr Brueton looked at me as if to say, are you quite sure? I thought again, and reached the same conclusion. Dr Brueton's expression was still doubtful, but sympathetic. He was probably thinking, this poor mother is so besotted with her daughter that she hasn't noticed how the baby's changed.

Perhaps I hadn't noticed. In the last month, she had undergone such metamorphoses that I could hardly remember what she was like before. I had seen Nella as the sickness took hold, her eyes huge and dark with great shadows beneath them, her skin waxy and yellow, her life draining away. Then I had seen her purple and bloated, the unconscious centre of a tremendous effort to save her life. Yet despite the immense and unimaginable things her body and mind had been through, here she was: bald and fatter than before, but – it seemed to me – extraordinarily unchanged. As soon as Clare turned up I asked her what she thought. She said she hadn't noticed any regression, and Kinta and Antony agreed with us.

Despite the fact that Kinta usually did the first two hours, the evenings were long in hospital. Antony and I would drive back there after a quick supper at home, and after he had played with Nella for a little while, he would then drive Kinta home. I pottered around the room, tidying things up, checking Nella's ileostomy dressing (which I could now change myself), and playing with her. At about nine o'clock, she was ready for sleep. I covered her with her cotton shawl – the room was so hot she needed nothing else. Then I would shake a few drops of lavender oil on a handkerchief tied to the top of her cot. This aromatherapy oil, bought in the local health food shop, claimed to have soothing properties which would waft infants into a peaceful sleep. I don't know whether it helped Nella but it always made me feel better, and the nurses remarked on how cool and fresh the room smelt.

I turned out the lights, but it was still too early for me to go to bed; so I brought the chair to the door, and wrote up the day's events in my diary by the light of the corridor. Sometimes, when I had finished, I would turn to the smooth, empty pages beyond and find myself straining to read what had not yet been written. It seemed so strange that the mind can cast itself into the past with such ease, and yet cannot go forward.

I went to bed around ten. I was tired, but I could not relax myself enough to give in to sleep. I felt like a person who wakes early in the morning, knowing the alarm clock is about to go off: the delicious languor of being in bed is ruined by the thought that one will soon have to get up; and I could expect to get up four to six times every night to soothe a fretful Nella back to sleep.

Our day started early. I rose at seven, drained Nella's ileostomy bag and changed her nappy. At half-past seven came the morning meeting in the sister's office. Each patient was then allocated to a new nurse, who was briefed on her charges by the nurse who had tended them during the night.

If the day-nurse had not worked with Nella before, she always took the trouble to introduce herself; and if she was one of those with whom I was familiar, she'd pop her head round the door and say something like, 'Isn't it nice – I'm looking after Nella today.' I liked the way they were so punctilious about these little courtesies. It was a way of saying that they recognised how much Nella meant to me, and an assurance that they would take good care of her.

Then the new nurse would take Nella's temperature and blood pressure, and put a urine bag on her – always a fiddly job, to which Nella took great exception. After a while, I learnt to do it myself, while the nurse held her legs.

I was usually up and dressed before Antony made his morning telephone call, and then I would make myself a cup of tea. The doctor who came to take blood appeared at about eight. As soon as he or she arrived, I went to find a nurse to hold Nella and comfort her. By the time I came back, Nella was whimpering, knowing what was coming. I gave her a kiss, told her to be a brave girl, and hurried out of the hospital. I felt doubly heartless; not just because I was abandoning her, but because I knew that had Nella been old enough to beg me to stay, I could not have gone. As it was, she was still too small to express her need for me – though no doubt she felt it just as strongly.

Beyond the Vauxhall Bridge Road, vast and windy as a motorway, was an intimate little shopping street with stalls selling fruit and vegetables. Having bought some fruit and a croissant I would hurry back to the hospital with my breakfast. Nella's blood had usually been taken by the time I returned – if I could still hear her crying, I bolted back downstairs again. By the time I did come up, Nella was so pleased to see me that I think it wiped the previous ten minutes clean out of her mind. She purred and cooed as I kissed her damp cheeks and dried her eyes. I marvelled at how forgiving she was.

Then I went to make myself some coffee. I always told Nella where I was off to and how long I'd be, although if something else was absorbing her attention she would not bother to look up as I left. I returned with the coffee to eat my breakfast, which Nella showed no signs of wanting to share. The TPN made her feel full all the time. Or had the shock to her gut been such that her appetite had simply vanished? My mind was more likely to dwell on trivial thoughts like this than the grim reality of her illness.

There were several reasons for this, one of which was that Nella herself seemed so unconcerned. Her development was unimpaired, and her bad days could usually be attributed to a collapsing vein, or sore skin around the ileostomy – in other words, to the treatment rather than the disease.

When something becomes routine, it becomes normal and loses its power to frighten. I had become so used to seeing Nella attached to tubes that it was easy to forget why they were there. I also had a subconscious feeling that after what had been done to Nella, fate could not be so cruel as to force her back into surgery and cripple her life. The EGF, as rare and valuable as a magic potion, must heal her. It would be too unfair if it didn't.

Living in this sort of mental cotton-wool took no effort, for I was emotionally and physically exhausted. The pill-induced sleeps I took during the day did not make up for the long succession of broken nights. Yet reality was never far away, ready to plunge me back into uncertainty at any minute.

Dr Sullivan took another biopsy on the fourth day of the

EGF treatment, and another the day after it finished. I noticed that he seemed more guarded than he had been a week ago.

'When will we know how her gut has responded to the treatment?' I asked.

'Well, not until we have all four biopsies back from the lab. In a week or so – perhaps a bit longer.'

Now I was nervous, on the alert. Last week he had talked of getting the slides back from the lab in forty-eight hours.

'Surely the one you and Antony looked at last week has come back, hasn't it?'

'Remember, we really can't tell anything from just one biopsy. It's only when we see them all together, as a sequence, that we can judge how the gut is progressing. I was going to send the samples to the lab one by one, as I took them . . . but on reflection, it's safer to send them all in a batch. There's less risk of them getting lost. Then I want Professor Wright to see them – as I told you, he is following Nella's case.'

'But things still look encouraging, don't they?'

'Oh yes. Definitely grounds for cautious optimism . . . However, I think I'm going to approach ICI again, and ask them for another six-day course of EGF.'

My blood froze, and for the first time in many days I felt fear and panic welling up inside me.

'Does that mean that the course of EGF she has just completed hasn't worked?'

'As I said, we won't know how well it has worked until we have the biopsies back. All the outward signs are encouraging.'

He would not be drawn any further. I felt like an inexperienced player watching a game of chess: he was thinking three moves ahead when he moved a piece, whereas I could only see the board in relation to what had gone before.

I returned to Nella, picked up the cotton animals and put them back in their pockets. She started pulling them out again. She seemed so calm and happy; yet how much longer would we have to be here if the EGF did not work, how much more pain would she have to bear? She would have to have that dreaded operation, the first of a long series. I imagined taking a pale little girl back into hospital for the third or fourth time, and her whimpering 'I want to go home, Mummy, please, please let's go home.' I couldn't think about it for very long.

In the meantime, there were other problems. The pattern of Nella's temperature was rising, which indicated infection. The most likely cause was the long line just beneath her shoulder. This carried only food, which is always vulnerable to bacterial invasion. However, the line had been put in under surgery and was supposed to last several weeks. It would not be removed until every other possible source of infection had been ruled out.

At eleven o'clock that Saturday night, four days after Nella was moved out of intensive care, a woman doctor I had not seen before came into the room and told me she had to take some blood. Nella was fast asleep, and woke up crying. I found the night-nurse who agreed to stay with Nella, and then banished myself to the furthest corner of Room One.

When the doctor came back into Room One with her cardboard tray, she told me she had the blood; but Nella had thrashed around so hard that the cannula in her hand had come out and had to be replaced. The doctor collected more equipment and went back down the corridor. Although I put myself as far out of earshot as possible, I was still listening hard for Nella's cries. They seemed to be going on and on, like an animal in a trap.

I became very tense and angry, and went downstairs to

call Antony. I woke him up and spilled out all that was going on in a tearful, gibbering voice. Talking to him made me feel better, though I have to admit that part of my relief came from sharing it all with him – in other words, trying to make him feel as bad as I was feeling myself. Antony was very concerned and suggested driving round at once; yet even I realised that there was no point in his doing so, for it might all be over by the time he arrived.

I went back to Room One, where the doctor was telephoning the registrar.

'Hello, Dr Nathan? Yes, it's me . . . I'm in Room Eight on Nathan Ward, trying to put in a cannula. I've tried three or four times now . . . I'm sorry to trouble you, but I feel it's just not fair on the baby for me to carry on.'

'Now she's a sensible one,' said one of the nurses in a low voice. 'Some of them would just keep jabbing away at the poor lamb.'

Dr Nathan Hassan was usually known as Dr Nathan, so as not to confuse him with another Dr Hassan who also worked in the hospital. He had a short black beard, and a Mutant Ninja Turtle clung to his stethoscope – put there, he told me, by his young son.

Dr Nathan was famous for his skill in finding veins. He always took time to examine every possible site. Only then would he prepare the needle and, like a water-diviner, he seemed to home in on the vein with some sixth sense. By the time Nella noticed what was happening, it was all over.

Her right hand, which had held the previous cannula, had been wrapped in bandages for so long that it now smelled distinctly cheesy. Before Dr Nathan left, I managed to wring a promise from him that if Nella needed another cannula over the weekend, he would come and do it. With a sigh, he agreed. There were fewer doctors at weekends, and the most experienced ones seemed to shoulder more than their fair share of the problems arising on Saturday and Sunday nights.

I remember expressing my admiration for Dr Nathan to one of his younger colleagues. I said I wished I could keep him in a cupboard like the proverbial bank manager, ready to spring out whenever Nella needed a new line. 'Yes, he is brilliant,' said the young doctor, 'but there's only one way to get that good: experience. He's been a paediatrician for ten years longer than I have.'

It was now around one o'clock. I tried to settle Nella to sleep, but the alarms on the pumps which regulated the intravenous feeding kept going off every time she moved and the noise made her more and more restless. The night-nurse thought that the long line was deteriorating.

The nurse went to call Frances, who was the sister in charge that night. Frances had a short pony tail and an athletic walk. She soon arrived and looked at the pumps and the line. One could see a sharp bend in the steel tube, just where it joined the bit that looked like a rawl-plug; and the point of entry was looking sore and red.

'Yes, it does look a bit dodgy,' she said. 'We'll give her some paracetamol, which should calm her down.'

However, I was the one that really needed calming down. The last two hours had left me feeling as if several layers of skin had been stripped off me, and I was obsessed by the possible removal of the long line.

'Supposing it packs up altogether?' I asked querulously. 'What will you do? Will they have to put in another little line, to carry the food? I couldn't bear going through all that twice in a night.'

'Look, don't worry. If you can settle Nella without her moving around too much, there's no reason why the long line shouldn't last till morning.'

'It's impossible to settle her without her moving around!' I snapped. 'And even if I did, she's only got to shift in her sleep for those damned machines to start bleeping, and then she'll wake up, and by that time the paracetamol will have worn off, and she'll start thrashing around again. There's no way that long line is going to last till morning, I know it, and I just can't go through another bout of digging for veins.'

Frances was not impressed. Her voice hardened.

'Look, I know it's difficult, but you've got to pull yourself together. If you carry on like this, you might as well go home – you're doing no good either to yourself or to Nella.'

Luckily, Nella was very tired. Frances arranged her comfortably and put out the light, and I was left in the dark, gently rubbing Nella's back. When I was sure she was asleep, I found myself a couple of aspirins and went up to the kitchen to make myself a cup of tea. I took it back down to the sister's office immediately opposite our room, which I often used as a reading room if it was empty. I sat down, furious and miserable. Why couldn't they have waited till morning to take the blood? Every nerve in my body felt tight as a wire, and I had not even been with Nella while she endured it all.

I had never been so oppressed by the long hard slog ahead as I was that night, and by the thought that if the EGF did not work, it would wreck my life as well as Nella's. I would have to endure this half-life for year after year, a prisoner of the hospital. I thought about the long hours still ahead, the endless succession of weary nights that stretched into infinity. I felt utterly defeated, for I realised at that moment that I simply didn't care about Nella any more. She was only an appalling imposition, an iron ball, to which I had been unjustly chained.

Frances came in, and sat down beside me.

'You mustn't take things so hard,' she said gently, 'or you won't be able to cope. You must try and accept the fact that babies just don't respond to pain the way we do. It doesn't stay with them in the same way – as soon as the pain stops, they forget about it.'

'I know, I know. It's just that it's so dreadful to see her in pain that it leaches everything out of me ... I feel I've got nothing more to give Nella. I'm useless to her. I've dried up. There's nothing left.'

The tears started running down my cheeks and into my lap, and Frances squeezed my shoulder. She found me some tissues and sat with me for a while, comforting me. By the time she left, I was a little more relaxed, and very tired. I went back into the room, and looked in the cot. Nella was sleeping soundly on her back, her newly bandaged hand thrown out on the sheet. I could just make out her fingers, curled around the plastic splint.

CHAPTER NINE

THE indifference I had felt towards Nella in the darkest hour of the night before had melted fast; but I could not shake off the feeling of flatness and lethargy, of being tired all the time. Perhaps I would have recovered quicker if I had faced all the emotions churned up by the crisis, instead of bottling them up in one image which I could not bear to look at. I felt very feeble, especially when compared to Kinta. She was nearly eighty, yet she was always willing to drive to the hospital and sit with Nella for as many hours as I needed to rest.

When I returned to Nella's room on Sunday night, Kinta turned to greet me with a smile. Nella had had a very good day, and the central line was still pumping.

Nella slept extremely well. This shows how tired she must have been, for the silence of the night was broken by the infuriating sound of a car-alarm. At last it stopped. I drifted off and was woken again, this time by dreadful screams apparently coming from Vincent Square. They went on and on, manic and insistent; I lay in bed and imagined some poor woman being raped and tortured by a latter-day Jack the Ripper. I prayed that Nella would not wake up and expected to hear police sirens at any minute. Why didn't they come? The local police station was on the west side of the square, barely seventy yards away.

The screams finally got me out of bed and I went to make enquiries in Room One. The sister on duty told me not to worry; the sounds came not from the square, but from the general paediatric ward on the floor below. One of the young patients was evidently very distressed. Yes, but why was he or she in such anguish? Was it pain? She did not know. The screams petered out eventually. I got to sleep around five, just as Nella was waking up. I spent most of Monday at home, feeling so tired and flat I could barely lift my body off the bed, every limb seemed like lead.

Despite the antibiotics, Nella's temperature continued to fluctuate, and it was established beyond doubt that the long line was to blame. The invading bacteria had colonised the inside of the line itself, so antibiotics could not reach them. On Tuesday morning, the doctors decided to remove the infected long line and put in a new one, on her other shoulder. This was only a minor operation, from which Nella suffered no ill-effects.

Dr Sullivan and Dr Brueton had also decided that the time had come to reintroduce food, in the form of peptides or elementary milk – also known, less attractively, as pre-digested milk. This would help the healing process, by stimulating the natural action of the gut. Like a muscle, the gut atrophies if it is not doing what it is designed to do.

On Wednesday morning, Nella's elementary milk was sent up from Pharmacy. I felt immensely proud that from now on, Nella would have her own little bottle in the fridge, properly labelled with her name and the date, alongside all the other babies' bottles. It was an enormous step forward – she was joining the ranks of normal children again. While I found and washed a plastic baby spoon, the nurse carefully siphoned the dosage – about two teaspoonsful – into a syringe. We then went back to Nella, who was sitting in her chair. She watched with interest as I poured out the milk: it had a thick, rather sticky consistency, yet looked more watery than ordinary milk. Gingerly, I lifted the spoon towards her mouth – and to my astonishment, she leaned forward, mouth open, to meet it. She looked surprised by the taste, but she cannot have found it unpleasant for she took another spoonful after that. Encouraged, I tried some myself: it smelt like button mushrooms, and tasted of mild soap and margarine.

The ileostomy meant that the little doses of elementary milk that she took by mouth only went through the upper part of the gut, before being decanted, with her other gastric juices, into the ileostomy bag. From now on, a certain amount of the fluid collected in the bag would be introduced into the lower section of her gut through a catheter held aloft by a nurse. Since it did not hurt, Nella was quite indifferent to the new procedure.

The yellowish-green, cloudy liquid was supposed to make its way into her gut by gravity, and occasionally it did. But more often than not, the nurse found herself holding the syringe in the air for fifteen minutes before so much as one teaspoonful had seeped in. The problem was solved by straining the liquid through several layers of sterile gauze, a job I often did myself, though it always made my stomach turn a little. Once cleared, the liquid flowed through the catheter quite easily.

Compared to the rigid protocol that was observed, and the immense care taken to keep everything sterile when it came to changing Nella's intravenous lines, I was surprised by how few precautions were necessary when putting things into Nella's gut – which was still the most badly damaged organ in her body. Naturally, I washed my hands before straining the liquid from her stomach, and the gauze was sterile. Yet the little foil pudding basin into which I drained it, and the catheter, were washed out with only soap and water. The catheter was used twice before being discarded. In between, it lay coiled in the basin like a slow-worm, with a tissue draped over it.

One Saturday afternoon, about a month after the onset of Nella's illness, I walked up the Fulham Road to our local library. I was still groggy after my late-morning snooze at home and was thinking vaguely about the next book I was going to borrow, when a grey Volkswagen came screeching to a halt beside me. It was Antony, driving Kinta's car, and for a moment I was rather alarmed – but the exultant smile on his face dismissed all fears at once.

He jumped out of the car, shouting 'You won't believe this, it's happened! They're growing!'

'What are growing?'

'The villi in Nella's gut! Dr Sullivan came, and he's got the biopsies back. He's looked at them, Professor Wright's looked at them, and there's no doubt about it – the EGF has worked! The villi are growing again!'

My spirits soared with relief and release. Laughing and hugging each other, we drove home. It was the best news we could ever have dared to hope for, and this time I had no scruples or superstitions about sharing it with everyone I could get hold of.

That night, Antony and I had the happiest supper together since Nella had become ill. On previous evenings, we had drunk wine to relax and dull the edge of our anxiety. Tonight, it was to celebrate.

The days wore on, though the knowledge that the EGF had worked made my semi-hospitalisation much more bearable. I sometimes found myself thinking about actual dates: would we be out by Christmas? I knew these were dangerous reflections and pulled myself back with the thought that Nella's time in hospital would last as long as was necessary: not a minute more or less.

I was no longer part of the world, but part of an institution. The polished parquet floors reminded me of boarding school, as did the fire alarms, which were set off at regular intervals to make sure they worked. My inner map had completely shifted. The hospital, not home, was the place I started from and came back to.

Kinta now stayed at our house in Fulham during the week, which was a tremendous help. She moved into Nella's room and took over the shopping. Soon the house was redolent with the herbs and sauces of her Tuscan cooking. She or Antony used to relieve Clare for an hour or so at lunch-time; sometimes, Clare was relieved by my mother, or my sister-in-law Sheila.

Yet in spite of all its comforts, and the presence of Antony and Kinta, home seemed strangely empty – and would remain so until Nella was safely back. It was no more than a filling station, a pit stop, an office, a darkened room with a bed in it. Room Eight on Nathan Ward was the centre of my life, but even there I was living like an evacuee, surrounded by plastic bags of things I had to take home, and lists of things I had to bring back.

I do not know how I would have managed without Kinta, and Clare. I also had the emotional support of a loving husband, and of my mother and father, who lived within a few miles of the hospital. I had no other children to worry about, and thanks to my sympathetic publishers, work had been easily set aside. Compared to the other mothers on Nathan Ward, the mechanics of my life were easy.

In the room opposite us were Rita and her baby daughter Stacey. Stacey had been born with hydrocephalus – water on the brain – and was then about three weeks old. Both Rita's older children had been born with the same condition, which had been corrected by surgery. The operation was equally successful on their younger sister.

I used to envy Rita, because she could walk up and down the corridor with her baby in her arms. She jiggled the baby gently and incessantly but neither of them seemed to enjoy it. Stacey cried, and Rita's impassive face bore a look of absent-minded resignation. Sometimes she looked angry and tired, but she never spoke roughly to the baby. In our brief conversations in the kitchen, I found out that her family lived in St Albans. The radio was her only distraction, since the television in her room didn't work. She was with the baby night and day, except when she went up for a quick cigarette and a cup of coffee in the Parents Unit.

At the other end of the corridor from us, in the room nearest the intensive care unit, was a Muslim baby called Fawzi. He had been born with an inability to swallow, which meant that his food could only reach his stomach with the aid of a naso-gastric tube. Fawzi was a great favourite with the nurses, who felt sorry for him because he was on his own for much of the day – his mother had several other children at home. Feeding him was a long and laborious job. The nurse held him on her lap, with a syringe of feed attached to his tube. Fawzi would make curious snuffling, gagging noises while it was going down, but he did not seem to mind very much. I expect he was just happy to be cuddled.

His mother came to visit him several times a week, and while she was there he was never out of her arms. She wore a thick headscarf which came low over her forehead, and was often accompanied by a man with a neat white beard, wearing a round white Muslim cap and a tunic over baggy trousers. My only view of them was a fleeting glance through the open door of Fawzi's room, as I walked to or from the kitchen. I often met the man's eyes, which were cold and distant. He and the woman always seemed to be sitting in silence. Was he Fawzi's father, uncle, grandfather? I expect the nurses knew, but they were not supposed to talk about the other patients, so I didn't ask. Fawzi's mother seemed very reserved, although she would occasionally smile at me shyly in the corridor. One day I saw a child's picture in Fawzi's room. 'THIS IS OUR HOUSE' it said in shaky capitals, and underneath was a pink square with a triangle on top for a roof. 'FOR FAWZI WITH LOVE FROM LEILA.' I suppose it was from his elder sister. I was told that Fawzi would probably not leave hospital until he was at least two, and could talk. Only then could a therapist teach him how to swallow.

One evening, I heard unfamiliar voices in the corridor. A tall man in a raincoat and a slender, tense-looking woman were walking up and down, talking earnestly. I thought at first that they were speaking Italian, until I found I could not make out a word they said. The man carried a large baby with pale skin, moon-like eyes, and a cranium buckled into a series of dips and bumps. Beneath the wispy hair I could see huge semi-circular scars. He and his mother were installed in a room at the opposite end of the corridor from us, facing Fawzi's.

We then overheard the couple talking to the nurses in heavily accented English, and learnt that they came from Yugoslavia. Their baby's name was Filip. (It is a curious fact of life on a neo-natal ward that one learns the name of a baby, who cannot talk, before one learns the names of its parents, who can.) The man stayed for a day or two, during which time doctors were in and out of the room all the time, holding long and earnest discussions. At every opportunity, the father walked up and down the corridor with little Filip in his arms. Then he went back to Yugoslavia. After that we sometimes saw Peter Fellows, the chaplain, walking around the ward with Filip so that his mother could have a few minutes to herself.

The following evening, Kinta came to sit with Nella while Antony and I went out. There was a telephone in the corridor, for incoming calls only. We had given its number to several members of the family, and the calls were often for us; so when Kinta heard it ring, she got up to answer it.

A nurse got there first. The call was for the Yugoslav mother. Kinta was struck by how desperately anxious and lonely she looked. She was a beautiful young woman, but there were deep shadows under her eyes. Her shoulders seemed pathetically thin, and hunched with sorrow. Kinta followed her back to her room.

'Excuse me,' she said. 'I just wondered if there was anything I could do . . . Can I help you at all?'

The woman jumped when she heard Kinta's voice, and then shook her head sadly. 'No . . . Thank you.'

Kinta went back to Nella's room, but she kept thinking about the Yugoslav mother. Then she had another idea. We had packed a picnic supper and a bottle of wine for Kinta, since we were going to be late that evening. She took the bottle, fetched a couple of glasses from the kitchen, and knocked hesitantly at the open door of the woman's room.

'I have some wine. Will you have some with me?'

Again the woman shook her head, and Kinta walked back down the corridor with the bottle and the glasses. She had just sat down again when the Yugoslav mother appeared at the door, a faint, shy smile on her face.

'Excuse me . . . May I say yes? I would like a glass of wine, please.'

'My dear, I'm so glad you've changed your mind,' said Kinta warmly. The woman looked relieved to have found such a kind and friendly soul among all the strangers that surrounded her, but she was still very reserved. Kinta found herself talking more about Nella than about Filip; but over the next few days, we learnt a little more. The mother's name was Nives, and she and her husband Tom came from Zagreb, in Croatia. When still in the womb, their son Filip had been diagnosed as having water on the brain. Since then he had undergone six operations. Then they heard about the Westminster Children's Hospital in London, which had pioneered a new technique for treating hydrocephalus. With the help of their families, they had managed to raise the money to bring Filip to England.

I remember seeing Nives just after Filip had been taken

down to surgery. She was sitting in a chair by the door, the empty cot behind her, twisting a small handkerchief in her hands. Her face looked more pinched and shadowed than ever. I knew what she was going through, but I had not had to go through it alone. I squeezed her shoulder, and told her we were all thinking of Filip.

The operation was a success. The new scar was tiny compared to the others on Filip's head, and he recovered well. Tom reappeared a day or two later, and Nives looked much happier – but their problems were not yet over. Filip was due to leave the hospital on a Friday, but his surgeon wanted to see him for a couple of check-ups, just to make sure that everything was all right before he went home to Yugoslavia. Tom and Nives therefore had to find accommodation for the following week.

Tom spent two days going from agency to agency, trying to find somewhere suitable. It was pouring with rain. The agents were sour and unhelpful, and the only places they could offer in his price-range were miles out of town. The landlords also demanded huge deposits, and a month's rent in advance.

By Thursday afternoon, the couple were desperately worried. They were due to leave hospital the following day. They had nowhere to go for hotels were prohibitively expensive, and it was still much too early for Filip to undertake the journey back to Zagreb.

With Kinta staying in our house, we had no spare bedrooms, but I told Nives and Tom that I would telephone a few friends. Someone might have a room for a week. I could not promise anything, but it might be worth a try. First of all I rang my father, John Julius. He and my step-mother Mollie have a spare room and bathroom in the basement of their house in Maida Vale, but it was often occupied by friends passing through London, or Mollie's younger, more nomadic children.

We were in luck – the room was empty, and John Julius and Mollie said they would be happy to let my new friends have it for their last week in London. I hurried back to Nives and Tom, and gave them the good news. It was a joy to see the look of relief on their tired faces.

I went home to fetch Nella's travel cot and push-chair, which Filip would use during the coming week; and that afternoon, I took them to see the room. It was not very large, and the two beds plus a cot took up almost all the available space; but it was quiet and looked out on to the garden, and Tom and Nives were delighted with it.

That evening, Mollie, Antony and I had dinner with them in a Turkish restaurant in Maida Vale. John Julius was giving a lecture, so he could not come; and Kinta had kindly volunteered to stay at the hospital, to sit with Nella and keep an eye on Filip. I was very sorry that they could not be with us and see the transformation in Tom and Nives. It was the first time they had been able to relax and enjoy themselves since coming to England, and the food, wine and company revived them. Tom, hitherto so reserved, became smiling and animated, and the lines of sadness and anxiety vanished from Nives's beautiful face. We asked them about Filip, and what they had to tell was a revelation.

Towards the end of her pregnancy, the Yugoslav doctors had told Nives that her child would be born with water on the brain, and would need immediate care. He was delivered by caesarian section two weeks early, and was whisked into an intensive care unit before she had a chance to see him. He was totally isolated from his mother.

'But that's monstrous!' I burst out.

'This is the normal way, in Yugoslavia,' said Nives, with a wry smile at our astonishment. 'I could only look at him.'

'Even that was not allowed,' said Tom. 'But I am in business. Import-Export. I brought perfume and whisky for the nurses, and they let us see him through a window. He

97

was in a big room, with many other babies.'

'When did they let you take him home?' I asked.

'For the first six months of his life,' said Nives, 'Filip was at home for three weeks only. All the time, he is in hospital.'

'And they never let you see him?'

'When he was out of intensive care, yes – I can see him one hour a day, no more. He was very ill, and always the operations, one after another . . .'

'Why did he need so many?'

'We don't know,' she said simply. 'In Yugoslavia, the doctors say nothing. You cannot ask questions.'

'We were told that Yugoslav hospitals are very high standard,' continued Tom, 'and the surgeon who operates on Filip is the best man in Yugoslavia, in all Europe. This is all we hear, so we accept. Then a friend of ours, a doctor, told us about Westminster Children's Hospital. She helped us with letters, forms, arrangements. Mr Lawson, the surgeon who specialises in this operation, he agreed to take Filip as patient and operate – but it is very, very expensive.'

We learnt that the hospital room alone cost them £230 a night, quite apart from the surgical and medical expenses: a small fortune in Yugoslavia.

Nives took up the story. 'It is so expensive we thought, this must be a beautiful hospital, very modern, with all modern things . . .'

I imagined what she must have expected: a high-tech palace of glass and marble and gleaming chrome. The Westminster Children's Hospital was built in 1907, and looks its age. Its grimy red-brick walls, adorned with Italianate reliefs of swaddled infants, must have come as quite a shock. Nives smiled at the memory.

'We took a taxi from the airport. When the taxi stop at this place, we thought he made a mistake, we thought this was . . . how you say, where they put children if their parents die.'

'The orphanage?'

'Yes, orphanage! But the taxi-driver says this is the Children's Hospital. We go inside, and everything is so old, so ugly. Artemis, I tell you, I could not believe my eyes. All our efforts, so much money, and we arrive in this old place like an orphanage . . . I sat down with Filip and cried.'

They were taken up to Nathan Ward, and the tiny room she had to share with Filip was no more encouraging; but Tom and Nives soon discovered what most people in this country know by experience: that you can't judge an NHS hospital by the state of its decoration.

'Before, in Yugoslavia, all Filip's operations were emergency,' said Tom. 'They wait till he is in critical condition, then they say we must operate now, immediately, this minute. Here, the doctors prepare him for the operation. They do tests, observations. When Filip is strong, blood pressure OK, not too much pressure in the brain, then they operate. We had never seen that before.'

Tom was also very impressed that the doctors took the trouble to talk to him and Nives, and explain what they were going to do. This was very different from the Yugoslav doctors, who neither expected nor encouraged questions.

'If you say, "How is my son? What is happening?" they become angry. They say, "Look, your baby is in the best hospital. We are doing our best for him. You can do nothing here, so go home."'

This attitude of cold indifference was shared by the nurses who looked after the babies.

'The nurses are told, it is bad to hold the babies more than necessary. If you do they become difficult, they do not sleep. So they pick them up, feed them, put them back in bed.'

'And what were the babies like?'

'They never cry. Just sleep. Filip was like that also. He was not used to contact with anyone, so he did not care if I was

99

with him or not. Now he is much better, he responds to me. And the nurses here – they play with him, they want to hold him! I could not believe it, it's fantastic. I have never seen nurses behave like this before.'

It seemed to me astonishing that, in the latter half of the twentieth century, there were still hospitals whose idea of a 'good' baby was one which had been denied all human contact, and had retreated into itself in black despair.

We returned to the hospital later than intended, and at the door of Nella's room, Tom and Nives said goodnight. Then Antony turned to Kinta, and apologised for having kept her so long.

'Not at all,' said Kinta. 'Nella's been asleep for the past hour, and I've been very happy with my book. I'm glad you all had such a good time. And as for those two,' she nodded up the corridor, 'I've never seen them looking so well.'

Nives and I kept in touch, and a year and a half later, she brought Filip back to England. He was due for a follow-up operation, to lengthen the shunt that prevents water building up around his brain. John Julius and Mollie lent them the downstairs room again, after their two-day stay in hospital.

Nives was as beautiful as ever, but tired, for life in the new republic of Croatia had not been easy. As for Filip, I would never have recognised him. From a silent, moon-faced baby with a buckled skull, he had grown into a lively two-year-old with mischievous eyes. I stroked his thick blond hair; his head looked, and felt, as smooth and well-shaped as Nella's.

CHAPTER TEN

NELLA had now been in hospital for five weeks. The doctors never spoke in terms of dates, which allowed too little room for set-backs. They preferred using well-worn phrases that parents could interpret as they wished. At first, we had been 'flying by the seat of our pants', and then for weeks we were 'not out of the woods yet'. Every day, I hoped to be told that there was light at the end of the tunnel; but those comforting words remained unspoken.

I was tidying the room one evening while Pam – the sister on duty – was passing the contents of the ileostomy bag through the catheter. Pam had a quiet, rather businesslike manner, yet when she smiled her whole face lit up. She was a great favourite of Kinta's. Nella started coughing. This did not alarm me much; but the cough became more and more throaty, and all of a sudden she began to vomit. I held her over the basin – the lines just stretched that far – and she retched again and again. I felt pitched back in time to that terrible evening when she first became ill, and my breath came short and fast with fear.

Thank heaven Pam was on hand. Her calmness reassured me, and she went to fetch a doctor. He arrived almost at once, and said she might have a viral infection – one of her ears looked a bit pink. We tidied up the bed and settled Nella, who went peacefully to sleep.

Two nights later, the same thing happened again only more violently. I was surprised at the amount of fluid she brought up, but it was clear. The doctor who came to see her was Dr Isabel Margesson. She had thick dark hair, glasses and an accent which was, I think, Brazilian. She often came to take Nella's blood in the morning, and was familiar with her case. At present, she was more concerned by Nella's rising temperature than with the contents of her stomach.

Isabel left the room and came back with the familiar little cardboard tray. By now, I knew what this meant. On this occasion, I did stay with Nella while blood was taken from a vein in her hand. I think I knelt behind the cot, holding her other hand through the bars, with my face close to the top of her head. I talked to her all the time, and watched her chest going up and down like a pair of bellows with short, hard sobs.

'Just in case the long line is infected,' said Isabel, 'I'll take some blood from there too.' This involved detaching the feeding tube from the line, and the usual precautions had to be taken to keep everything sterile. Then she attached a syringe and drew blood up through the long line, while I held Nella still. When the blood was taken, she reattached the tube.

'Look, there's an air bubble in the feeding tube!' I said anxiously. 'Isn't that very dangerous?'

'Well, it can be dangerous if it's a big bubble,' replied Isabel, 'but I think I can break this one up.'

She found the small plastic clamp that hung like a clothes-peg on the tube, and snapped it on so that the bubble would not pass into Nella. Then she flicked a finger gently and repeatedly against the long plastic tube. The bubble broke up, but four inches back, another bubble appeared. She flicked this, and the bubble divided in two. Several more bubbles had appeared up and down the line before she went to call for another doctor.

The next doctor to arrive was Tim Hall, who was on Mr Tabara's surgical team. His manner was detached and ironical, and he hardly opened his mouth when he spoke –

which sometimes made him hard to understand. He had no better luck with the bubbles than his colleague, and they both agreed that the lines should be changed. This meant disconnecting the feeding containers and their tubes from the connecting tap (which Isabel had just done, when she took blood from the line) and replacing them with new ones. Hospital rules dictated that this job should be done by the charge nurse, who is usually the sister in charge of the ward; so they asked Nella's nurse to call her.

The charge nurse that night was David. He came from Sheffield, and had a comfortable, cheery presence that children responded to immediately. One night, he had found me reading *The Songlines*, and it emerged that he had a passion for travel. Like many people who become nurses, he liked the idea of belonging to a profession that was welcome anywhere in the world.

David came into the room, and the doctors asked him to change the TPN lines.

'Sorry, I can't do it,' he said. 'I'm agency. This has to be done by a sister on the hospital staff.'

The doctors groaned.

'It's late,' said Tim Hall, 'and she can't go for long without new lines. Couldn't you . . .'

'I'm sorry, I really am, but those are the rules. Now if you'll excuse me I've got to get back to Room One. Shall I telephone Robert Mond Ward and ask the sister there if she can come up?'

'Don't worry, I'll call her myself.'

I looked at David's retreating back in astonishment. Here was Nella, in need of new TPN lines, and there was David, an experienced charge nurse who had done the job a thousand times before. How could a liberated, well-travelled man like himself, I thought, stick to stupid rules at half-past ten on a Saturday night? I turned on Isabel, as though it were her fault.

'This is ridiculous! Why won't he do it? We might have to wait for hours for a sister from another ward!'

'It's to do with insurance,' she sighed, 'and a critical shortage of staff. David was right to refuse – he is bending the rules already. As an agency nurse, he should not even be in charge on this ward. The rules say that every ward in this hospital should be in the charge of a sister on the hospital staff. But at the moment, there are not enough sisters on the staff for basic requirements.'

When Amanda told me about the strain that staff shortages placed on her, I was very sympathetic; but now that they were affecting me, I saw the nurses and sisters in a less charitable light. As Nella whined and grizzled, I imagined myself losing patience and stamping off to Robert Mond Ward in a towering rage – though it would hardly have done much good. It was the weekend again, when the hospital was always under strain.

My fumings evaporated as soon as the sister arrived, looking tense and apologetic. She had not expected to take so long, but one of her patients had needed urgent attention. She and the doctor looked at the lines again. The biggest bubbles had vanished, and the little ones were now too small to bother about. On reflection, they both decided that the lines should stay in place after all. It was midnight, and the last two hours had been a complete waste of time; yet irritation was tempered by the thought that we could at last go to bed.

I settled Nella, put out the lights, and dozed off. An hour later, we were woken again – it was time for Nella's antibiotics. The stinging sensation as they went through the new line in her hand seemed to upset her more than usual, but at last that too was over, and I was left to try and get her back to sleep.

Nella was restless, and her crying became increasingly plaintive and agitated. In the darkness, I could see her picking and pawing at the long line, which was not like her. I turned on the lights, and saw that the dressing on her shoulder was oozing a pinkish substance – a mixture of TPN and blood.

I hurried up the corridor and found David, who came at once and examined the dressing. 'Looks like it's leaking. The long line will have to come out.'

'It only went in about ten days ago. I thought they were supposed to last for weeks.'

'Well, that's the idea . . .' He stroked Nella's head. 'You're having a rough ride tonight, aren't you, little one? I'll go and fetch the doctor.'

Half an hour later, Isabel arrived. A trolley with disinfectants and sterilised equipment in plastic pouches was wheeled in, and the doctor put on rubber surgeon's gloves. Then the thin, four-inch-long steel line was carefully drawn out of Nella. I held her jerking arms, with my head close to her screaming face – her smooth cheeks shook, and my cheek became wet with her tears and sweat. She relaxed as soon as the line was out, and lay gasping for breath while I dried her face. Then I was shown the line, which lay on a piece of green disposable towel. It was as thin as a needle and threaded, like a metal guitar string, for strength and flexibility. Yet just below the rawl-plug-shaped entry point, there was a sharp kink – the site of the leak.

Nella was given some paracetamol, and once I had turned out the lights she soon settled down. Then I went downstairs and telephoned Antony. I knew it was past three o'clock, I knew he was working flat out; but I could not rest until I had told him the whole saga. I felt as irrational as a child, whose pain only goes when it has been kissed better. His love and sympathy were usually all I needed; but I must have sounded more desperate than usual tonight, for he said 'I'll drive over straight away.'

I felt too weak to say no.

Antony was with me in twelve minutes. We talked for a while in the sister's room. I was crying – again I felt so empty that I had nothing left for Nella. Antony said 'Look, you are so wound up I think you should go home. I'll stay here till Clare comes.'

'Are you sure?'

'Yes. I've brought a book. Can we call a cab from here?'

'I'll take the car, you don't want to drive it back in the rush-hour.'

'Do you think you can drive all right? You look very shaky.'

I said I would be fine. I dressed, said goodnight to Antony and Nella, and made my way gratefully downstairs.

As I drove home through the empty streets, I felt ashamed of my impatience towards the doctors and nurses that night. Each one of them was overstretched; yet I knew how hard they worked, with real commitment to the children in their care. The fact that Nella was not only alive but also recovering was proof of their skill.

On the other hand, to work day after day in a hospital built at the turn of the century and totally unsuited to the demands of modern technology was both tiring and demoralising. Everyone seemed cheerful enough, and there was no shortage of laughter and banter in the corridors. Yet on a deeper level morale was sinking, and everyone was aware of it. People did not stay long. Young nurses came to do their training in paediatric care, and moved on.

Part of the problem was that, with the hospital's approaching move to the new Westminster and Chelsea Hospital, there was little incentive to improve conditions. The senior nurses were consequently under tremendous pressure. Pam told me that in most hospitals, a clerk deals with the daily running of the ward – ordering stores, organising shifts and so on. At present, they had no ward clerks. So Pam had to spend the morning doing administration, which was a waste of her time, her training, and the tax-payer's money.

The net effect was demonstrated to me forcefully one day when, coming into Room One, I overheard the sister in charge on the telephone:

'The Emergency Bed Service, please. Hello, this is the Westminster Children's Hospital. I'm speaking from Nathan Neo-natal Ward. Just to let you know, we have no more high-dependency cots available at present ... Yes, we'll let you know when we do.'

'Why is she saying that?' I whispered to one of the nurses standing by. 'There are only two babies in here, and there's room for four!'

'You can't offer cots if you haven't got the nurses to go with them,' came the reply.

This is even more chilling when one thinks that each cot in Nathan Ward is at the top of a great pyramid of resources. By the time Nella arrived at the Westminster Children's Hospital, highly experienced medical and surgical teams were already on standby, armed with the latest technology and all the specialised back-up she might need. What would have happened if there had been no available cot in the intensive care unit of Nathan Ward, the day Nella became ill? Even if we had 'gone private', Nella would have been dead by the time a specialist had found a bed and put a medical and surgical team together.

Without a long line to carry it, Nella's TPN had to be dripped through the line in her hand. The little peripheral veins that took the line soon collapsed – they did not seem to last longer than thirty-six hours before someone had to come digging for a new one. To my relief, another long line was put in under anaesthetic, four days after the old one came out.

I prayed that this would be the last central line she would have, for there was now talk of reversing the ileostomy: in other words, of sewing Nella's gut back into one piece. The medical team were so satisfied with her progress that they told me there was a good chance of Mr Tabara performing the operation the day after his return from holiday. However, the decision on when to operate was his alone.

I waited for Mr Tabara on the morning of his return in an agony of suspense. Nella's skin had become very sore under the ileostomy dressing, and it would not have a chance to heal properly until her gut was joined up again. He came in around ten, with members of his own team and several doctors.

'Good morning. How is she doing, Mum?' asked Mr Tabara gravely. (He called all the mothers 'Mum': it simplified the whole problem of names. In the Arab world, women are often addressed as 'Mother of', followed by the name of their eldest child.)

I told him that Nella was doing remarkably well, and all the doctors agreed. Mr Tabara nodded sagely as we spoke. There was a short pause, and I plucked up courage to ask, 'When will you reverse the ileostomy?'

'I want to settle myself in first – perhaps next week. How long has she had it?'

Everyone tried to remember the date the ileostomy was performed, while the young doctor who held Nella's file – now the size of a large telephone directory – rummaged about among the papers. The answer was, six weeks.

'I prefer to wait seven weeks before reversing an ileostomy. Perhaps next Wednesday. Goodbye, Mum.'

They all trooped out, leaving me to contemplate the week ahead. Never have seven days looked so interminably long, and it seemed so cruel that Nella should be condemned to another week of soreness and discomfort. I imagined that the area around the stoma would look like minced meat by then.

The day after that, Nella had a loopogram, a test designed to reveal whether or not the gut has narrowed at any point — a potentially dangerous side-effect of extensive bowel surgery. In this test, Nella was first given a barium meal. To me, a barium meal was one of those medical processes that lie on the borders of nightmare, along with electric shock treatment and bone marrow transplants. I imagined it must be like drinking a glass full of mercury. The doctors, however, assured me that it was closer to a very heavy milk-shake.

I left before the test began, leaving Clare with Nella. Clare told me the barium was bright pink and strawberry-flavoured, and did look like a milk-shake; but apparently Nella was not impressed, and it had to be administered via a naso-gastric tube. Poor Nella. In intensive care she had almost got used to tubes being pushed down her throat, but once it was no longer a daily event it was terrifying. Clare told me that Nella was dreadfully upset, and retched violently. However, once the tube was in place she hardly minded the barium. A sequence of X-rays was taken of her gut as the barium passed through. As far as they could tell, Nella's gut had not narrowed at any point.

Amanda, the sister who had been with us the night Nella was admitted, had been away on a course. At about this time she came back to Nathan Ward; and when she saw Nella again, the smile of incredulous delight on her face was tremendously encouraging.

'I just can't believe it!' she exclaimed, gazing at Nella. 'I cannot believe that this is the same baby! It's amazing, it really is. In all my years of nursing I have never seen such a sick child get better so fast.'

Nella was getting stronger every day. One warm sunny morning, when Wendy was the sister in charge, she came in to see Nella.

'Isn't it a lovely day?' she said. 'If it's like this after lunch, I thought perhaps you might like to take Nella for a walk.'

'A walk! I didn't know it was possible . . . I suppose it's a job for two people, is it – one to push the push-chair, and one to hold the drips?'

'No, it doesn't have to be that complicated,' laughed Wendy. 'This is what happens. We have to change the lines once a day, which means detaching Nella from the drips. At that point you take her out.'

'What, like any other baby?'

'Yes, like any other baby. For an hour, mind, no more. And then when you come back, we'll hook her up again.'

I thought about the walk all morning. We'd go to St James's Park, feed the ducks, and look at the squirrels, and Nella would gaze at the animals as though seeing them for the first time in her life. At last, she would be a normal child again. That afternoon, I came back with her buggy.

Wendy and Nella's nurse came in with the trolley and the sterile pouches, and Nella's long line was detached from the drips. Then Clare and I dressed her up warmly, put her in the buggy, and went downstairs.

Nella sat quite still and looked about her with huge, wary eyes. I was bursting with pride, and pushing her about through unhampered space gave me a feeling of tremendous exhilaration. Exulting in freedom, it was as if I had been the one attached to a line for the past six weeks. Clare and I walked across Vincent Square, up Horseferry Road, across Victoria Street. We were constantly pointing things out to the little invalid – 'Oooh, look at the big red bus, Nella! Did you see the big black dog?' – but I think the world looked younger and brighter to us than it did to her, for soon Nella was fast asleep. We woke her up when we got to the bridge over the lake in St James's Park, and I held her while Clare threw bread for the ducks. Nella peered downwards and watched the sleek birds churn the water as they darted this way and that for bread. She seemed interested, but not as delighted as I had hoped she would be.

Time flew by quicker than I thought. Rather than stay out one minute after the allotted hour, we took a taxi back to the hospital — and then Nella really did wake up. Her face alight, she whooped and gurgled at the scene passing by. The taxi-ride was unquestionably the high point of her first excursion, and it put her in a good mood for the rest of the day.

This surprised me. I thought she would not like returning to the hospital, and being tethered to her cot by the lines once more; yet she looked quite relieved to be back in her room again, and went peacefully to sleep that night. The walk seemed to do all three of us so much good that we were allowed out again next day, this time with Kinta. It was much colder, and we did not go so far. We bought Nella an absurd white bonnet with a huge pom-pom on it, in Tachbrook Street Market.

That Saturday night, an agency nurse whom I had not met before was put in charge of Nella. When she came in to read the drips she seemed quite oblivious to Nella and me, and crashed about with a torch as though searching for a gas-meter in a dark cupboard. She took far longer than usual to read the drips, and then stomped out without attempting to close the door. I leapt out of bed and closed it hard behind her. A few minutes later she was back, with a bigger torch. Without a word to me she went back to the drips and studied them again. Then she ripped a green paper towel out of the dispenser, and started scribbling on it. By now I was furious, but said nothing: if I did, I knew I would be ruder than I meant to be. Again she walked out leaving the door wide open, and the only reason I did not slam it behind her was for fear of waking Nella.

Soon afterwards, Nella became very restless, and seemed to be running a fever. Usually, I would tell the night-nurse; but this time I went straight to the sister in charge. I would have told her what I thought of Nella's nurse there and then, but since she was not alone I thought I'd wait. I don't think the sister had much confidence in Nella's nurse either: she walked straight past her in the corridor.

It was not until we were safely in Room Eight that I relieved my feelings.

'That woman shouldn't be allowed in a neo-natal ward!' I hissed. 'She's about as sensitive as a bulldozer, and I don't think she can even read the drips!'

The sister looked more sympathetic than I had expected, as she took Nella's temperature. 'We are very short-staffed,' she explained. 'The agency sent her to us at the last moment. At the weekend, we have to take whoever we can find.' Then she glanced at the drips and frowned. 'I'll be back in a minute.'

She came back with a paracetamol suppository, and Nella's fluid chart. She did some sums, and corrected the figures on the pumps.

'What's the matter?' I asked anxiously. 'What has she done?'

'It's all right, don't worry. Try and get some rest. I'll look after Nella for the rest of the night.'

The reassurance that Nella was in competent hands dispelled my anger. She went peacefully to sleep, and the sister came in to read the drips during the night as quietly as a shadow.

Next morning, the day-nurse told me what had happened. In the space of two hours, the night-nurse had allowed six hours' worth of lipids (the white intravenous food which contains fats) to drip into Nella. A doctor assured me that she would suffer no ill-effects as a result, and that that particular night-nurse would not be coming back. As Nella seemed comfortable, I was content. There was no point in dwelling on what might have happened; and the single bad experience I had with one nurse only served to increase my admiration for all the others I met at the Westminster Children's Hospital.

On Sunday night, Nella was sick again. At first, it was just water, and I was not very concerned; but with each retching the fluid turned darker, and with mounting terror I saw it become brown and viscous, just as it had in that dreadful dawn when we realised how ill she was. I thought that something terrible must have happened inside her gut, that this was the beginning of a new crisis. Would she have the strength to fight for life all over again? I was back on that nightmarish mental roller-coaster, lurching between hope and despair.

We went through the same cycle once more. Her temperature soared, blood was taken, another course of powerful antibiotics was prescribed. Her throat looked very red, and everyone hoped and prayed that this was the source of the infection.

Monday night was very hard. The last dose of antibiotics had to be infused into Nella over·the course of one hour, and the process was not over till two in the morning. We both went to sleep, but at four I was awake again. Nella was whimpering, her whole body flushed, hot, and trembling. The doctor who came to see her said that the infection was most probably in the long line; but he had instructions to keep the line in place for a further twenty-four hours, just in case the antibiotics brought the infection under control.

On Tuesday morning, her temperature was back to normal, but I waited for the doctors in great trepidation. I knew that if her temperature started to rise again, indicating that the antibiotics had failed to kill the infection, Mr Tabara would not operate the following day. His day for surgery at the Westminster Children's Hospital was Wednesday. If he did not operate tomorrow, we would have to wait another week for Nella's final operation – a prospect I found almost unendurable.

113

The doctors were still not absolutely certain that the long line was the cause of the infection, but they decided to take it out. 'A difficult decision,' said Dr Sullivan, 'but probably the right one.' If the long line were responsible, Nella's temperature should drop at once, and the operation would go ahead. If it were not, the line would have been pulled out for nothing; Nella would still have an infection; and the operation would most probably be postponed another week.

It all depended on how Nella's temperature reacted over the next twenty-four hours.

Chapter Eleven

NELLA was very restless that Tuesday night, tossing and moaning incessantly. I got up again and again to try and settle her, thinking she was awake – yet she was fast asleep. I was at the end of my tether; the broken nights and desperate worry of the last few days brought back that feeling of exasperated indifference – I felt I had nothing more to give her, that she had taken everything from me. At half-past two I changed her nappy, then her ileostomy dressing.

Her temperature rose only a little in the night, but the following morning, David was making very discouraging noises. He thought it unlikely that Nella would undergo surgery today. The CPR levels in her blood, which indicate infection, were extremely high.

The thought that her operation might be delayed for another week was profoundly depressing. However, a little later Trotty, the anaesthetist, came in to see Nella.

'Doesn't she look wonderful?' said Trotty, beaming into the cot. 'When I think of the first time I saw her . . .'

'Is she well enough for the operation?' I blurted out anxiously. 'What about this CPR level?'

'I'm not worried about it,' said Trotty. At once I felt better. 'But of course, the final decision is Mr Tabara's.'

Trotty left, and my spirits sank again. I must have looked pretty gloomy when Brenda came in a few minutes later.

'Are you worried about the operation?' she asked.

'I'm frightened it might be postponed. Trotty is quite

happy, but Mr Tabara is so scrupulously cautious ... he's bound to postpone it another week.'

'Not necessarily, you know. It's generally the anaesthetist who holds back. If she's willing to go ahead, that's usually good enough for everyone else.'

Brenda was right. At eleven o'clock Nella was detached from her lines, and I carried her down in the lift to the operating floor. All I could see was blue lino, white walls, and closed doors. I put on a gown, and elasticated plastic covers like shower caps were slipped over my shoes. People in blue gowns came and went, and we were led into the operating ante-room, where Trotty presided over a small group of nurses. I put Nella down on the couch. She was very upset by all the gowns and bright lights. She might not have known where she was, but she knew she had been there before and it was a strange and frightening place. Trotty had to put a cannula into her hand, to take the anaesthetic, and I bent down to be as close to Nella's head as possible. I heard Trotty saying, 'This won't take long.' Nella was crying. Then there was a little sigh, then silence. Her eyes were open, but unseeing.

'Don't worry,' said Trotty. 'I'll take care of her.'

Nella was now sufficiently strong that I was not in the least worried about the operation. Yet I had been warned that she might have to be put on a ventilator afterwards, for after heavy anaesthetic many babies have difficulty in regulating their breathing. I could not get this thought out of my head. Again and again I imagined Nella waking up to the horror of a tube being pushed down her nose, unable to control her breathing, retching and struggling.

I often thought how strange it is that, despite the extraordinary advances achieved by modern medicine, the technology to sustain the body's systems is still so invasive. No matter how sophisticated the pumps and monitors, nor how

skilled the doctors and nurses who use them, the front line –
where technology meets patient – is still painfully simple.
TPN goes into the body via a needle stuck into a vein. Blood
must come out the same way. Air must go into the lungs
through a tube pushed deep into the throat.

The anxiety of the last two or three nights, the febrile
activity of getting in and out of bed all the time like a
jack-in-the-box, had reduced me once again to sleepless
exhaustion. As soon as I had delivered Nella safely into
Trotty's hands for the operation, I went home, leaving Clare
to sit with Nella when she came up from surgery. I took a
couple of sleeping pills and went to bed.

I called Nathan Ward as soon as I woke up, and spoke to
Clare. She reassured me that all had gone well, and no, she
had not required the ventilator. This was a tremendous
relief. I snuggled back into bed, knowing that Clare would
be relieved by my aunt Atalanta at six, and that I had
nothing to do but sleep.

That night, Antony and I went out for a long-standing
dinner engagement. Knowing that Nella was recovering
well, I enjoyed myself very much; but I was longing to see
Nella again, and left early. Antony stayed on, for the guests
of honour had been brought together as a direct result of
his research into the Battle of Crete.

I drove back to the hospital and raced up the stairs to
Nathan Ward. To my horror, her room was empty. Did that
mean they had had to put her on a ventilator after all? I
hurried on to Room One, feeling sick with apprehension;
but there she was, breathing deeply and quietly all by
herself, with my aunt Atalanta reading beside her. They had
put her in the intensive care room purely as a matter of
post-operative routine.

I had the delicious luxury of sleeping alone in Nella's
room that night. Nella was wheeled back the following
morning, and Antony suggested that he do a night at the

hospital. I accepted with alacrity. Nella was very grizzly that afternoon and I thought he would have a terrible night with her.

As it turned out, Nella slept soundly, but Antony's night was still sleepless. He was not used to the disturbances every few hours, and to make matters worse, he had a bad back at the time. By morning, he felt that a night on the floor might have been preferable to the tortures of the fold-up bed.

Nella's gut was now all in one piece, and only the scars remained on the surface of her abdomen. With great satisfaction, I took the bags, flanges, powders, ointments and dressings that were used to take care of the ileostomy, and returned them to the store-room behind Room One.

Dr Brueton, Dr Sullivan and Mr Tabara all came in one day, and pronounced themselves very satisfied with her progress. They beamed into the cot where Nella, wearing a white T-shirt, was playing with a cloth ball. A few weeks ago, her chances of survival had been very slim indeed; yet thanks to their efforts and her own strength, here she was, almost well again. For a moment they stood watching the infant in silent wonder, like the Three Wise Men.

Bowel sounds are the first indication that the gut is recovering from post-operative shock. The doctors were always listening to Nella's abdomen with a stethoscope, like they do with pregnant women, but for three days they heard nothing. She was often sick. A great deal of poison-green fluid was coming up from her stomach with considerable violence. It looked very alarming, but I was assured that this was quite normal. Soon the fluid became so copious that a naso-gastric tube was put in, and the fluid was drained out with a syringe every once in a while.

Despite her progress, it was a stormy week − for Nella had no long line. There were no plans to replace it: the doctors anticipated that she would soon be feeding herself. Until that day, however, Nella's TPN would have to be pumped into her through peripheral veins.

I was grateful that Dr Nathan Hassan was most often called to find new veins – yet even he had trouble during these last few days. Once again, he was obliged to site the cannula in a vein in her scalp. The next line was sited in her foot. I woke that night to hear her crying: the bandage on her foot was sopping wet with TPN, tinged pink with blood.

On Monday, 22 October, exactly eight weeks after her arrival in hospital, Nella had her first bowel movement since the reversal of the ileostomy. All the doctors were very excited. Dr Nathan Hassan came in with his stethoscope. Leaning over Nella, he announced 'Yes! I can definitely hear propulsive bowel sounds!'

I laughed, thinking he had said 'repulsive'.

He grinned back. 'PRO-pulsive, not RE-pulsive! Anyway, they are the right sounds. Well done, Nella! I expect she'll be back on elementary milk tomorrow.'

Later that day, Dr Sullivan said there was light at the end of the tunnel. Here at last was the phrase I had been waiting for so long, and in Nella's case the metaphor seemed particularly apt. However, my happiness was tempered by the fact that there was still a great deal of fluid in Nella's stomach. Mr Tabara did not rule out the possibility of blockage, due to adhesions; but his first idea, to stop draining the liquid, proved correct.

The reason was simple enough. Immediately after the operation, Nella's gut – still in post-operative shock – had not been able to cope with all the fluid in her stomach. She was often sick. At that point, draining the fluid off had been a good idea. Yet now that the bowels had recovered, that fluid was needed to stimulate them into action. The siphon was draining it off before it could be absorbed.

I decided the time had come to move out of Nella's room. Wendy and Frances, and Kinta and my mother, had all said that sooner or later I really ought to get Nella used to the idea of sleeping alone again. But I felt guilty about it, perhaps because I wanted to leave her, wanted to sleep through the night for a change. At the same time, I wanted to stay in the hospital. That way I could be with Nella morning and evening, while only having to make the journey to and from home once a day.

Now was the ideal time to make a move, for three reasons. The first was that a bed on the Parents Unit had become vacant. The second was that I had developed a streaming cold, which I did not want to pass on to Nella. The third reason was Sas, the night-nurse.

Sas was short for Saskia, and she came from New Zealand. She had short fair hair and an upturned nose. She was very fond of Nella, whom she spoke to in a cootchy-coo voice which Nella adored. Nella also loved her bungey plastic name-badge, which became a nightly treat. 'Here, chicken,' Sas would say, 'will you look after this for me?' Nella took the badge and sucked it until bed-time, when she was only persuaded to part with it in return for a dummy. Sas had been on nights for the last week, and would be doing at least one more week.

'You have a few nights' rest, and leave her to me,' said Sas. 'We'll get along fine without you, won't we, chicken?'

I did not leave Nella until I was sure she was asleep; then I tiptoed out and said goodnight to Sas, who promised to call me if Nella became unhappy. Then I went up to the Parents Unit. I shared the room with a mother called Sarah, who was a non-smoker like myself; but our room was next to the smokers' sitting-room. There was a strong smell of cigarettes, and we went to sleep to the sound of voices and television jingles; but compared to a night with Nella, this was peace indeed.

I rose early and hurried down to Nathan Ward. Nella was still asleep.

'How's she been?' I asked Sas.

'Fine, just fine,' she replied. 'We had a cuddle after her two o'clock obs, and she hasn't woken up since.'

Nella now began taking elementary milk again. It was flavoured with blackcurrant and was a lurid puce colour, which she liked at first but went off fairly rapidly. For the next two days, peptides were introduced via the naso-gastric tube. Her bowel absorbed them well, and on Thursday she was deemed ready for a half-and-half mixture of water and baby formula milk. Again, the gut absorbed it well, but Nella did not like it at all. When she would not take it from a bottle, I persuaded her to try a little from a cup. She took the cup from me, and raised it to her lips – then started gagging.

When I told the doctors they sighed, but were not surprised. The truth was that Nella had forgotten how to eat, and if she did not remember soon, a speech therapist might be called in. I was told that speech therapists know all about the muscles of the face, and can sometimes be very effective in cases like this.

It was all taking much longer than they had expected, though overall they were satisfied with her progress so it did not really matter – except for the frequency with which new veins had to be found to carry the TPN. I felt that every time they dug for a line the experience must be worse for her – that the effect was cumulative, like shell-shock. Yet I don't think it was like that for Nella. She lived exclusively in the present. Each time blood was taken or a new cannula put in, the experience was painful, but fresh – not made worse by anticipation or memory.

And compared to some of the treatments other children were undergoing, Nella's was not so bad. Sarah, with whom

I shared a room in the Parents Unit, had a son, Timothy, who was a dwarf. He was undergoing extensive surgery to lengthen his legs. This was done by breaking the thigh-bone and setting the break with a small gap: both ends of the bone then grew towards each other, making the new bone longer. The flesh and muscles, too, had to be lengthened. The process was painful and tedious, but Timothy was determined to see it through. He was ten years old. He would go through the same operation again at the age of fourteen, and after all those weeks of hospital and nights of pain, he would be four inches taller. It did not sound like much to me, but it was to Timothy.

Sarah sat with him every day, from morning till nine or ten at night. The family lived in Warwick, and could not visit every weekend. Sarah had two other children. She worried about her daughter, who was preparing for her GCSE exams, and wished she was back at home.

For the couple from Bahrain, who were also long-stay visitors in the Parents Unit, home must have seemed as distant as another planet. Neither of them spoke any English, and the woman was always wrapped in a long black cloak. One day, I said 'good morning' in Arabic. After the initial shock of surprise they both beamed with pleasure, took me by the arm, and sat me down on the bed in their room. They soon discovered that 'good morning' was about all the Arabic I knew, but we always greeted each other in the corridor from then on. Their son Karim was the boy undergoing chemotherapy, whose courage the nurses so admired.

By Friday, the doctors decided that Nella was ready for full-strength baby formula through the naso-gastric tube, and the gut absorbed it well. That evening, when Antony and I went back to the hospital as usual, Nella was grinning at us from the cot and waving her arms; and as I smiled at her, I was only vaguely aware that the room looked larger and lighter. Then Kinta, who had her back to us, turned round with a joyful smile on her face.

'Look! Do you see? They've taken away the drips!'

It was true. The black hat-stand, the drips, the pumps, the lines – they were all gone, leaving Nella with nothing but the naso-gastric tube. I could hardly believe it – I picked Nella up and hugged her, with tears in my eyes.

'When did it happen?' asked Antony.

'At about three this afternoon,' said Kinta. 'And you won't believe it, but when they took all the equipment away, Nella started crying. They had been her companions for so long, I think she felt quite lost without them.'

'And has she taken any food since then?'

'Yes! I managed to persuade her to take twenty-five mils of formula, from the bottle!'

This was the most that Nella had ever taken since she became ill. We hugged the triumphant Kinta, and gazed at Nella in wonder, as if she had climbed Mount Everest.

I lifted Nella out of her cot, and Antony and I took her for a walk down the corridor to celebrate. We walked up to Room One and I looked at the place where she had once lain. Her ghost was still there: swollen, purple, soiled with dried blood and sweat, with peeling skin and moulting hair, tubes and wires winding over her body like snakes; but I held the real Nella, a warm, clean, delicious baby body next to mine. Her hair was starting to grow again. It smelt of ironing boards and digestive biscuits, just as it should.

Once the TPN was stopped, Nella began to feel the pangs of hunger – and the memory of how to eat returned. She still did not drink as much as they would have liked, but this was made up for by pouring the required amount down the naso-gastric tube. On the following Monday, Nella was reintroduced to solids – sloppies really, made of baby-rice and formula milk. She liked this far more than milk by itself, and her interest in drinking – which was very feeble – positively slumped.

The following Monday, Nella's naso-gastric tube was removed; for the first time in eight weeks, her own body was supporting all its systems without help. She was complete, fully mobile, and watertight.

Her last night in hospital was on Tuesday, 30 October. One last test, we were told, and then – if the results are satisfactory – she can go home on Wednesday.

The test went by the magnificent name of Cellobiose Mannitol. This determines the permeability of the small intestine, one way of assessing its integrity. It involves taking a urine sample after four hours of nil-by-mouth; then the patient takes a measured amount of xylose; and the first urine passed after that is collected and analysed.

It sounds simple enough, and is, when you are dealing with an adult patient; but after four hours of nil-by-mouth, Nella seemed incapable of having a pee. Finally she did, and then a naso-gastric tube was put down her nose to administer the xylose. Poor Nella – after her few blissful hours of tube-free life, she must have thought the torture was starting afresh.

Now all that remained was for Nella to pee again. By three o'clock she was still dry, and getting very hungry and thirsty. Her pathetic wails touched my heart and I began to seethe with impatience and irritation. Soon, even the hospital staff got tired of waiting and thought no harm would come if they put some water down the naso-gastric tube. Then I noticed that the urine bag was half-off. I removed the whole thing and was just reaching for another when Nella delivered an absolute torrent of urine which drenched the bed.

I nearly cried with vexation. Nella, too, was distraught

with fatigue and hunger. At last, at five o'clock, she peed again. I have never felt such a sense of profound relief – it was like a shackle suddenly falling off, and all my irritation was instantly dispelled.

The naso-gastric tube came out for the last time. We gave Nella some rice and milk; then we dressed her, and took her once more into Room One to say goodbye to Wendy, Brenda, and the others. Our goodbyes were brief, for they were busy preparing for a new emergency patient who was due to arrive by ambulance at any minute.

Walking out of Nathan Ward with a healthy baby in my arms made me feel profoundly happy, but there was a sense of sadness too. This hospital would always be a part of me. I had lived through the worst moments of my life here, and some of the best. Yet as Clare and I walked downstairs, my joy swelled and I began to feel so triumphant and glorious that it made me quite nervous. Nella might still develop adhesions, and if she did we would be back in hospital again. The happier I was now, the harder it would be to come back.

I strapped Nella into her seat in the back of the car, and Clare climbed in beside her. By now it was rush-hour. Since we were stuck in traffic in the King's Road, I had plenty of opportunity to look at Nella. She was gazing out of the window, her face lit up by the lights of the shop-fronts. She seemed utterly bewildered, quite silent, passive.

We arrived home at seven, to be greeted by Antony and Kinta who had been preparing for the home-coming. Nella was still very quiet. We took her up to her own room, and set her down. She looked around, eyes alight now, and started the soft cooing noises that she made when she was happy.

However, I still had a great deal to worry about as I put her into her cot that night. Nella was very peaceful and content; but she was still not drinking as much milk as she ought, and I was haunted by the spectre of kidney infection brought on by too little fluid in the body. I also feared that she would not sleep. She had been so used to the noise and interruptions of nights on Nathan Ward that her own room must have seemed as dark and silent as the grave.

To my amazement, Nella slept for a full twelve hours, barely moving. I should have slept too, but I couldn't. My mind seemed unable to leave the hospital. I went over and over the events of the last few weeks, and fretted about kidney infections and adhesions. Both Antony and I were worried by Nella's silence. We got up several times during the night to make sure she was still alive. I had a nightmare that she had been abducted by a group of cat-footed Satanists who had slipped in through the bathroom window.

It took several days at home before I could accept it was all over – it was a bit like adjusting to peace after returning from a war. For the next few nights Nella went on sleeping the sleep of the innocent, her breathing so calm and deep it was barely audible. Antony and I could not resist creeping up to look at her, back in her own wooden cot again. It was an image that neither of us had dared dream about.

CHAPTER TWELVE

FOR the first three days after we got home, we continued to worry at how little Nella was drinking. She was refusing the hospital's brand of powdered baby formula, so Antony had the bright idea of putting her back on the one she had had since birth. From then on, she never looked back. Every day she ate and drank a little more, and the threat of kidney infection faded away.

I took her back to the hospital for regular check-ups; first they were once a week, then once a fortnight, then once a month. After every check-up, I went up to Nathan Ward with Nella. She would cling to me, silent and apprehensive; but the nurses who had looked after her loved seeing her again, and even those who had not were curious. On one occasion, a new doctor asked what my baby was called.

'Eleanor,' I said.

'Not . . . Eleanor *Beevor*?'

'That's right.'

The doctor looked quite star-struck, as if she had just been introduced to Shirley Temple.

Nella often suffered from nightmares, particularly on the nights after a check-up. All children have nightmares; but I felt that with everything she had been through, Nella's were perhaps more realistic than most. Her terrified screams always woke us, and Antony would dash up to her room. The sooner he arrived, the sooner he could settle her; but sometimes the nightmares were so vivid that I would have to join him, and rock her for several minutes before she was willing to go back to bed.

These were the only ill-effects she suffered, and they were very transient. Mine were not so dramatic, but they were long drawn out. For months I felt emotionally pulverised. The slightest reverse became a crushing blow, even if it was something as insignificant as running out of bread. Christmas shopping left me in such a tangle of indecision that I seized up altogether, and had almost no presents to give.

My energy level had never been so low. The slightest task seemed to require a superhuman effort, and everything seemed pointless. I lost interest in my work, found it difficult to concentrate on anything, and worried about everything from Nella's diet to our financial future.

I knew this was an understandable backlash; I had been warned that I would feel very depressed and run down for a while, and up to a point I was prepared for it – but at the same time my weakness and lethargy made me very irritable. With the help of all our family and friends, I had had more support than anyone could have hoped for in hospital; and best of all, Nella was alive and completely cured. I had nothing to worry about and everything to be thankful for. Antony was my greatest comfort, for he understood the bleak despondency that overwhelmed me from time to time. He encouraged me to rest, and always managed to coax back a calmer and more positive frame of mind. He too could take things a little easier. He had delivered his typescript on time.

In early January, I began writing an article for *Harpers & Queen* about Nella's time in hospital. For the first time in weeks I was able to concentrate. This was very encouraging, and the writing itself was therapeutic: in reliving what had happened to Nella, I began to face up to all the emotions I had run away from at the time.

The possible development of adhesions was still a danger, and a few weeks after we got back from hospital, Nella woke up screaming with stomach cramps in the middle of the night. We rushed her round to Nathan Ward, but by the time we arrived the seizure had passed – it had evidently been no more than a bad attack of wind. The following morning Peter Sullivan rang to find out how she was. I assured him she was fine, and apologised for the false alarm; but he repeated that we should not hesitate to bring her round if her health ever gave us cause for concern.

In the late spring, we found ourselves rushing back to hospital in the middle of the night once more. This time, Nella had a very high temperature, and she was shivering uncontrollably. To my dismay, the doctor said he needed to take a blood sample. I did not stay with her but Antony did, holding her close and repeating 'It's all right, it's all right'. Nella, who was now starting to talk, took up the refrain and cried 'All right! All right!' throughout the ordeal, as if it were a healing mantra. The infection proved to be in Nella's throat, and she was in hospital for twenty-four hours. Every time a nurse came to take her temperature or a doctor approached, Nella would start whimpering 'All right, all right', as though the words would keep them at bay.

In June 1991, eight months after Nella returned from hospital, Dr Sullivan asked us to come and meet Professor Nicholas Wright, the expert on EGF. He was still working at the Hammersmith Hospital, but was now Director of Clinical Research at the Imperial Cancer Research Fund, which is where we went to see him.

As the three of us waited in reception, I imagined Professor Wright as a man in his mid-sixties, with grey hair, formal manners and half-moon spectacles. One of his younger colleagues would no doubt come and lead us to the great man's office; and sure enough, a door opened and a fresh-faced, energetic man of about thirty-five walked swiftly towards us. To my astonishment, this was Professor Wright himself.

He took us up to his laboratory, where he and his colleagues worked in rather cramped conditions. Work benches jostled for space with metal-shelving units piled high with papers and equipment. In the middle of the room was a long table, on which was a microscope. This microscope had four additional eye-pieces jutting out from the main body of the instrument, so that five people could look at a slide at once.

Professor Wright took us through the case, illustrated with the four slides of Nella's gut. These had been prepared from the biopsies Peter Sullivan had taken before, during, and after her six-day course of EGF. First we saw the extent of the devastation: the picture was mostly white, with a few trailing wisps of crushed and formless tissue. Thin, hesitant lines drifted into emptiness – the broken walls of dead cells. In the next three slides, things improved. 'Look!' said Nicholas Wright excitedly. 'Just to the left of that long bit which looks like a fish. That's the base of a new villus!' I could not always identify what was being pointed out, but even a non-scientist could see the improvement. The cells became plumper, their arrangement more organised and purposeful, and they no longer had broken walls.

I knew that I was staring at a sliver of tissue unimaginably small, and transparently thin; yet the image was of such complexity that it looked like a great landmass, photographed from a satellite suspended hundreds of miles above the earth. It seemed almost unbelievable that this was a particle of my own child, and that I was actually seeing the process by which her gut began to grow again.

Professor Wright then took us into his office at the end of the laboratory, which was occupied by himself and his colleague, Dr Robert Goodlad. He sat us down with mugs of coffee, and told us about EGF with scientific gusto.

In its natural form, it had been identified by Professor Stanley Cohen in 1963. Cohen found that it was produced in the salivary glands, and in some glands in the gut called Brunner's glands – it also occurs in mother's milk. The hormone had extremely exciting possibilities, for it made atrophied gut grow. In 1986 Professor Cohen was awarded the Nobel Prize for his discovery.

During the 1980s, the development of recombinant DNA technology allowed EGF to be made synthetically. It was manufactured by a small pharmaceutical company in High Wycombe, G.D. Searle, which provided Wright with the EGF he needed to produce his first paper in 1986. In it, he proved that the gut of a rat will atrophy if it is fed only intravenously; but if it is given EGF, also intravenously, the gut will start growing again.

EGF not only regenerates the gut; it also drastically reduces acidity in the stomach. ICI became interested, and set up a research programme. They hoped that this would lead to a new cure for peptic ulcers, a potentially huge market; but when it was established that oral ingestion of EGF was ineffective, and when the project leader retired because of ill-health, the project went into abeyance.

The fact that EGF does not work in pill form is a drastic limitation. Large pharmaceutical companies prefer to concentrate on drugs capable of mass oral consumption with huge turnovers, to finance research as much as to generate profit.

G.D. Searle, the company which provided the EGF for Wright's first paper, was bought out by the American giant Monsanto. All the scientists working for G.D. Searle lost their jobs, and the EGF molecule – the genetically engineered building block from which more could be made – was removed to the United States.

For Nicholas Wright and his team, it was a bitter blow:

without access to an EGF molecule, their work would grind to a halt. To construct an EGF molecule is an enormously long, complex, and expensive business. Once you have it, it can be made to reproduce on certain highly specialised yeasts. Wright compared the process to a very sophisticated beer-making kit. Only at this stage does EGF become relatively inexpensive to make.

The scientists previously employed by Searle founded a company called British Biotechnology, and negotiated with Monsanto for the return of the molecule. They succeeded in getting it back to Britain, and were willing to provide Wright with small amounts of EGF. But Wright wanted to get EGF into the clinical arena, where it would be used on humans; and for this, a special pilot plant would have to be set up. British Biotechnology could do it, but it would cost £100,000 and they could not make the investment themselves.

Wright then turned to the Imperial Cancer Research Fund, but although they supported his work, they could not provide the funds. He realised that the money would have to be raised, and that had been the main reason for inviting us to his laboratory. He had hoped that we might launch and organise an appeal fund to amass the £100,000 needed for the pilot plant.

'But you've been let off the hook,' he announced with great satisfaction. Antony and I asked what he meant.

Just a couple of weeks earlier, well after the date of our visit had been fixed, he had addressed the American Gastroenterological Association in New Orleans. His paper presented the latest work on EGF, leading up to a description of Nella's case – the first time that EGF had been tried on a previously healthy human gut. He showed them the slides we had just seen, which charted her gut's return from near destruction to healthy growth; and to underline the impact of her extraordinary recovery, his last slide showed the main photograph from the article in *Harpers & Queen*, of Nella in my arms.

At the end of the talk he was approached by Dr Ron Nardi of Parke Davis, a large American drug company based in Illinois. Nardi said that his company would be willing to supply Wright with EGF in grams – in other words, in industrial quantities. With the help of Parke Davis, Professor Wright hopes to begin the first clinical trials of EGF.

Antony and I left the meeting with a tremendous feeling of pleasure. Not only had Nella survived, but her case seemed to have done a great deal to encourage further research. I like to think that perhaps that image of a laughing one-year-old girl, in perfect health, might have had something to do with it. The work on EGF continues. Peter Sullivan will be going out to Hong Kong where, with the help of Parke Davis, he will be developing clinical projects to use EGF on certain neo-natal conditions.

Oblivious to these exciting developments, Nella is flourishing. At twelve months she started to crawl, and soon after that, she started to talk. She picked up new words with extraordinary rapidity, and could form simple sentences by the age of eighteen months. She had always been a big baby, and eight weeks in hospital did not curb her growth. She is now two, but looks more like a three-year-old.

Children seem to be born with sixty or seventy years of life-force packed into them. This is what makes them so resilient in sickness, so energetic in health. But I feel that some of Nella's life-force must have been used up in her desperate fight for life. Despite her size, she is not physically adventurous or athletic. She takes great care getting on and off the slides and climbing frames in the park. Like all children she is easily excitable, laughs and talks a lot, and loves being tickled. She hates loud noises, and does not bang things about for pleasure. Books are still her favourite toys, and she spends more time sitting on the floor than running around. She eats well, but seems to need a lot of sleep.

Nella still goes back to the hospital at six-monthly intervals. The doctors want to monitor her weight and look at her scars (Nella used to be frightened by this; now she thinks they want to admire her belly-button, and lifts up her vest with enormous pride). Yet I am more aware of the profound pleasure they get from seeing her just as she is: a normal, healthy child, playing with wooden bricks on the floor.

Every evening, at bathtime, I undress Nella and see the scars again; not only the big ones on her abdomen, but also the tiny white bumps that mark the sites of her neck-lines and long lines. There is a bluish spot just above the wrist on each hand, marking enlarged blood vessels below the surface. I do not find them upsetting, rather the opposite. They are the scars of a battle from which she has emerged triumphant.

Peter Sullivan once remarked, 'She is a miracle baby, you know.' I cannot forget it. The nights are no longer fraught with nightmare and anxiety; but every morning, when we go into her room and see her sleepy smile, the miracle repeats itself.